1400
99BB

THE
SEXUAL
MATRIX

Also by Sam Kash Kachigan

Sam Kash Kachigan is also the author and producer of the following books (B), software (S), films (F), and videos (V).

Statistical Analysis: An Interdisciplinary Introduction to Univariate and Multivariate Methods (B)

Multivariate Statistical Analysis: A Conceptual Introduction (B)

The Game: A Lesson (B)

The LENNOX System of Market Forecasting (S, V)

Doggedy Dog Dog (F, V)

The Mondo Bello Series (F)

THE
SEXUAL
MATRIX

Boy Meets Girl On The Evolutionary Scale

Sam Kash Kachigan

Radius Press

New York

THE SEXUAL MATRIX

No part of this book can be reproduced without the prior written permission of the publisher, RADIUS PRESS, P.O. Box 1271, FDR Station, New York, NY 10150.

Manufactured in the United States of America

Library of Congress Cataloging-in-Publication Data

Kachigan, Sam Kash.
    The sexual matrix : boy meets girl on the evolutionary scale / Sam Kash Kachigan.
        p.   cm.
    Includes bibliographical references (p.   ) and index.
    ISBN 0-942154-77-0
    1. Sociobiology.   2. Sex role.   3. Sex differences.
    4. Interpersonal relations.   5. Body, Human — Social aspects.
    I. Title.
    GN365.9.K33   1990
    304.5–dc20   90-60730
                                                          CIP

15 14 13 12 11 10 9 8 7 6 5 4 3 2 1

To my mother

About the Author

Sam Kash Kachigan was born in the United States of America of immigrant Armenian parents. He received his education at the University of Wisconsin-Milwaukee, the University of Washington, and Columbia University. He has held a variety of teaching and research positions at the university, corporate, and consulting levels. In addition to being the author and producer of several books and computer software, he is a documentary film maker with a special interest in beauty and nature.

Contents

Preface

This book will appeal to anyone interested in the behavioral differences between males and females; especially with respect to their mating dynamics in an evolutionary perspective, and the consequent implications for alternative population characteristics.

In content and approach the book is designed primarily for students of anthropology, biology, communications, political science, psychology, and sociology; whether at the introductory, advanced, or lay level. This broad audience is dictated by (1) the fundamental importance of gender differences and their implications for all aspects of our lives, and (2) the proposition that significant knowledge must necessarily be interdisciplinary in nature.

While poets and scientists have long studied the differences between males and females, the present approach differs considerably from their traditions, being neither prosaic nor antiseptic, but more in the nature of a bulldozer, by virtue of the belief that the ultimate goal of serious artistic and scientific effort is to lay waste to historical edifices of thought that are built on weak foundations, and to do so in the most efficient of ways. At the same time, I have not neglected the basic tenets of sound scientific investigation and logical reasoning; which automatically replace inadequate theories and ideas with fresh perspectives, laying new foundations for societal change.

To strictly categorize the book, it falls most naturally within the domain of sociobiology, a relatively new and broadly based discipline concerned with the biological foundations of behavior in an evolutionary context, first explicated by Edward O. Wilson in his truly monumental book *Sociobiology: The New Synthesis* (1975); where he has brought together the original evolutionary ideas of Charles Darwin, advances in genetic knowledge, statistical properties of populations and the environment, plus a wealth of additional theory and empirical data from the entire animal spectrum. Indeed, this integrated approach to the understanding of behavior will eventually make its greatest contribution by breaking down the rigid walls between conventionally defined disciplines, forcing a more global view of the behavior of animals and humans in their interactions among themselves and with the planetary environment as a whole.

It is in the above spirit that I have written this book. And though much of what I have to say has been said before (though not in the same permutation), there is a great difference between stating a proposition and teaching it, so I have resorted to every pedagogical trick to make my message more memorable; including operational writing, clarity, repetition, emphasis, pacing, metaphor, rapping and rhyming, diagrams, exaggeration, analogy, logic, examples, silliness and satire, anecdotes, and when all else fails, callous humor and the blunt statement of unpalatable facts—which particular combination, depending on the cosmic dimensions of the issue at hand.

At certain points in the presentation of gender differences, I may be overly harsh on certain factions of feminists, and that is only because I sometimes feel as if we are among families and children at the county fair, when a gang of these screamers commandeer the stage—venom dripping from their lips—indiscriminately blasting everyone in sight. It is not even the abrasiveness and inappropriateness of their approach that is so irritating, but rather the ill-defined, misdirected, and maladaptive nature of their nagging, taking on the characteristics of a collective neurosis. So when the empirical evidence overwhelmingly contradicts their "male-cultural-hegemony" mantra, I am forced to lay bare the fallacy in the clearest possible terms. In the end, though, I believe they will be among the staunchest supporters of this analysis, for it points the way to the solution of many of the major grievances of contemporary society—from any particular *gender* or *sexual affinity* perspective.

Other ideological groups will also be offended by the presentation. Indeed, many of the conclusions presented in the book are so far removed from contemporary thought—including religious, scientific, and governmental doctrines—that most individuals will be initially freaked out by them, especially when certain propositions are considered out of their overall context and logical development.

But I am confident that a unique minority of individuals will embrace the ideas presented in the book, and eventually make them more agreeable to all; with the attendant result that many of the major ills of contemporary civilization will become more transparent, and hence more amenable to change, creating a more positive world—the ultimate criterion for the validity of any form of communication.

Sam Kash Kachigan
April, 1990
New York

To raise good children,
We must bear good children.

—Rámana Rámanámana

THE
SEXUAL
MATRIX

Chapter 1

Gender Analysis

1. Introduction

There is perhaps no better way to understand human behavior as a whole than to analyze the differences between *males* and *females.*

This characteristic of individuals to be either male or female is referred to as the *gender* variable. An individual's gender is also sometimes referred to as that person's "sex," although this usage of the term *sex* to mean *gender* is imprecise and rapidly becoming outmoded, for reasons which will become apparent in our later discussion of sexual affinity.

Although humans differ on countless variable characteristics, their difference on the gender variable—being male vs. female—is the most fundamental of all human characteristics. Since each of us was born from a mating of our mother and father, and since we share many of their traits, an understanding of their behavior and what characteristics brought them together, is, in a very real sense, an understanding of ourselves and our own mating behavior.

More generally, an understanding of the differences between males and females has implications for all aspects of our existence, including the nature of our child-rearing practices, our education system, social conventions, the workplace, governmental legislation, and mating behavior itself, to name just some of the more important ramifications of a comprehensive understanding of gender dynamics.

The need for a fuller understanding of gender differences is especially important in this age when a significant number of females are voicing multiple grievances; complaining that they are being slighted by society and getting the short end of the stick in contemporary culture, which they often view as a male-dominated conspiracy against their happiness. Through a more thorough understanding of the gender variable, we will try to uncover the roots of these female grievances and perhaps to more effectively address their malaise, as well as that of the male population which has gender-related grievances of its own.

In the following sections of this introductory chapter we will outline the approach that we will take to analyze the gender variable, this most basic of all human characteristics.

2. Research Methodology

Population segments such as males and females are variously referred to as *in-tact, extant, correlative,* or *cohort* groups. Other examples of such groups include high school graduates and dropouts; conservatives, moderates, and liberals; heterosexuals and homosexuals; murderers and non-murderers;

Blacks, Browns, Tans, and Whites; Christians, Jews, Muslims, Buddhists, and Hindus; users and non-users of a product or substance; believers and non-believers in an attitude or fact; etc.

In each instance, membership in one group or another is dependent on some criterion, or standard of classification; which may be well-defined, as in the case of high school dropouts, and at other times it may depend on a less reliable self-description, as in political preference or sexual affinity. The nature of such groups will determine whether an individual can change membership from one group to another within the classification scheme. For analytical purposes the groups comprising a particular classification must be *mutually exclusive;* that is, an individual cannot belong to more than one group in the categorization.

These types of naturally occurring in-tact or extant groups are to be contrasted from *experimental* groups, which are purposefully created by the administration of alternative experimental treatments to randomly formed groups that are essentially indentical before the treatment. For example, a test drug vs. an inert placebo, or one teaching method vs. another, is administered to individuals in alternative groups *randomly selected* from a larger population. In the case of these experimental groups, the interest is on the treatment effects, not the groups themselves, which are deemed to have only minor random differences going into the experiment.

In the case of extant groups, in contrast, the interest is primarily in determining characteristics on which the existing groups differ, beside their defining characteristic. We search for these differences between extant groups mainly to flesh out a fuller picture of their discriminating traits and to understand their basic natures, most often to establish meaningful *societal policies* aimed at addressing the group differences.

For example, in what other ways do murderers and non-murderers differ, besides their murdering behavior? How else do school dropouts differ from non-dropouts? The answers to these types of questions help us to understand the groups and establish societal policies, and in some cases influence group membership or the behavior of group members. The more differences we can uncover, the more thoroughly we will understand the groups, and the more likely we can establish policies which address those differences.

The most straightforward way to study such groups—of which males and females are an instance—is to observe random samples of individuals in each group population and compare them on any number of characteristics deemed important. The measured characteristics might include membership in various other qualitative groups, or values on *quantitative variables* such as height, weight, grade point average, blood pressure, or annual income; the distinction between qualitative and quantitative variables resting on whether the defining *levels* of the variable differ in *kind* only—as with males vs. females of the gender variable—or differ in a rankable *quantity* sense, as with the levels of the height or weight variables.

The most common approach to studying global group differences is the *survey research* method, wherein well-structured questions are asked or large samples of group members, or information is gathered from reliable external sources. Information on the samples of individuals from each group are then compared to determine which other characteristics—besides the group defining characteristic—differentiate between the groups. This is done by comparing the groups with respect to their *average* scores, as well as the *variation* of those scores, on each of the measured variables. When many such variables are measured, it is also necessary to determine the *covariation* or *corre-*

lations among the variables in order not to be misled by seemingly frequent group differences among the many variables, which in fact might merely be reflections of themselves. With such an analysis we can then draw a picture of the variable characteristics that differentiate between our groups of interest.

For example, we might find that murderers differ from nonmurderers in the criminal records of their parents, or in the extent of belief in a particular attitude, or any of a number of other possible differences. Since we only study *samples* of individuals, rather than the entire *population,* and since the uncovered differences may seem marginal, statistical techniques must be used to decide whether the observed differences are reflective of true population differences, or if they are just chance or random fluctuations in our limited samples of data.

When reliable differences between groups are identified, some attempt must be made to coordinate those findings into some kind of coherent model or theory, providing a deeper understanding of the groups which will help to establish societal policies with regard to the populations in question, or, at the very least, to generate hypotheses for further research. More information on the types of analyses that are used to identify such group differences can be found in my textbook *Statistical Analysis: An Interdisciplinary Introduction to Univariate and Multivariate Methods.*

In our present study of the differences between males and females, for reasons which will become clear, we are not going to use the above quantitative survey approach. Such types of gender studies are plentiful and have provided a wealth of data on males and females. Too often, though, the differences that have been uncovered are often marginal, ambiguous, or at the very least have not been able to be formulated into a comprehensive theory of gender differences.

The current approach will be based on *personal observations,* an approach widely accepted in the fields of anthropology and sociology, but less so in psychology—my particular area of schooling—and often for good reason. Personal observation can be fraught with errors of selective notation, and its lack of large samples and quantification often makes valid conclusions illusory. More often, this observational approach, which is usually small in scale in terms of the number of persons observed—whether individually or in small groups—is most useful for *generating hypotheses* or nailing down the *variety* of variables that might be studied in follow-up quantitative research.

But our present observational research approach is considerably different from the conventional small-scale exploratory qualitative methodology. Rather, it is based on personal observations of literally *millions* of males and females over many decades, and is restricted to *dramatic gender differences in behavior,* differences which no one can deny, and therefore require no statistical hypothesis testing to affirm their reliability; only a theory to integrate and lend meaning to them.

The problem with many contemporary gender studies is that they are often too ambitious, trying to study abstract and complex forms of behavior such as *nurturance, leadership, moral development, empathy, charisma,* or *managerial skill;* concepts that cannot readily be defined, much less reliably observed and recorded. In contrast, we will be studying forms of male and female behavior that can be seen by all with total agreement.

Ultimately, the validity of personal observations, as with quantitative survey research or controlled experimental studies, depends on whether the observations can be *replicated* by other researchers. Here we stand on the firmest footing, for the forms of behavior that we have chosen to study are blatant in nature, and the observed gender differences in these behaviors are so dramatic that there can be no serious debate about their reality.

3. Behavioral vs. Biological Differences

Humans differ on countless variable characteristics, some of which are *biological* in nature, while others are *behavioral* in nature.

Among the biological characteristics on which humans differ are the variables of height, weight, blood type, various hormone and enzyme levels, as well as skin, hair, and eye color, to name a few.

There is also a large number of behavioral variables on which individuals differ, ranging from 100-meter running speed, to choices on various paper and pencil tests, to performance in various occupations.

In addition to biological and behavioral differences, we can also consider a third class of characteristics on which humans differ; namely, attitudinal and aptitude variables. *Attitude* variables have to do with differing *beliefs* among individuals on controversial issues such as capital punishment, abortion, and intoxicant usage. *Aptitude* variables, on the other hand, are concerned with the *potential ability* to perform various tasks, whether it be scores on a written test or walking a tight-wire.

But if we look more closely at these attitude and aptitude variables, they are not really a separate class of characteristics, for ultimately they must be manifested in *behavior* in order to be measured. We do not know whether someone holds a particular attitude on a specific issue unless they display some kind of behavior revealing that attitude, whether that behavior is the choice on a written questionnaire or calling someone a "dirty" name. Similarly, we cannot know whether someone has a particular aptitude—say, the ability to play piano—unless they demonstrate it with actual behavior.

So, we are left with our original distinction of differences among individuals as being either biological or behavioral in nature. Now just as the population as a whole differs on biological and behavioral variables, the subpopulations of males and females differ on these characteristics. Within the male population there are differences, and within the female population there are differences. For example, males differ among themselves in height, and so too do females differ among themselves in height.

In terms of gender differences, though, the concern is whether males—*as a group*—differ from females on a given variable such as height. When we say *there is a gender difference in height,* we do not mean that every male is taller than every female—for surely there are many females who are taller than many males—but that *on average* males are taller than females. Also, such groups may not only differ in terms of their average value for the variable in question, but also in their *variation* on that characteristic; that is, the shape of the distribution of scores. Groups can have the same average value on some variable, yet differ markedly in the variation of those scores—say, in terms of the relative frequency of extreme scores, whether high or low. See Figure 1.1 for examples of different types of population distributions.

There is no question that males and females differ on many biological variables besides height. Indeed, the gender variable itself—being male vs. female—is defined in terms of biology. While the distinction is often made with respect to cellular chromosome differences, most simply we can say that an individual born with a *penis* is a *male,* while an individual born

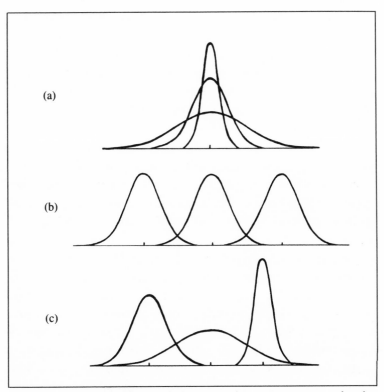

Figure 1.1—Distributions which have (a) the same average value but different variation, (b) different average values but the same variation, and (c) different average values and variation.

with a *vagina* is a *female,* with the recognition that there is a very small incidence of ambiguous instances of this definition; but our main interest is in rules, not rare exceptions, which only serve to prove the rule.

Aside from the defining biological distinction, males and females also differ on a variety of other biological characteristics, to a greater or lesser extent, some more widely acknowledged than others. These include anatomical, physiological, and neurological differences. Most adult females have distinguishable breasts, while males tend to have more facial and body hair. There are also skeletal and musculature differences between males and females, which are obvious by observing their profiles or gaits. Hormone levels and physiological functions related to the different reproductive organs also differ from males to females.

In short, there is a multiplicity of anatomical, physiological, and neurological differences between males and females. There are major differences in these areas that everyone agrees upon, and some less dramatic differences that most researchers agree upon, while other distinctions are too marginal for universal agreement.

While there is wide agreement that there are major biological differences between males and females, there is still a significant number of individuals who deny that there are also gender differences in *behavior.* And of those who admit gender differences in behavior, many attribute it to external cultural or environmental factors rather than to inborn *genetic* factors. A significant number of individuals believe that there are *no* inborn gender differences in behavioral potential.

This is the basic issue we want to address, for it is among the most important of all contemporary controversies, by virtue of the sweep of implications it has for every aspect of our lives. If males and females do not differ in their behavioral potentials, that is one thing; if they do differ, that is something else. The answer to this question has implications for the very fabric of our civilization, from mating, to child-rearing, to education, to the workplace, to societal legislation and government, to the very evolutionary course of the human species.

Our interest is in documenting gender differences in behavior and tracing them to biological underpinnings. To us, it would seem rather remarkable from the start, that given such dramatic biological gender differences, that they would not be manifested in behavioral differences as well.

Since there are many who agree with this position, and many who disagree, and yet others who are skeptical, our ultimate purpose is to influence this balance of belief in the direction of creating a consensus that can act in concert to address the many societal implications that it engenders.

4. Gender vs. Sexual Affinity

If all boys were sexually attracted to girls, and all girls were sexually attracted to boys, the separate variables of *gender* and *sexual affinity* would not be necessary; one would exactly determine the other.

While there is a strong relationship between gender and sexual affinity, these variables are to an extent *independent,* or orthogonal to one another. That is, whereas most males and females are sexually attracted to the *opposite* gender *(heterosexual),* a minority are sexually attracted to their *own* gender *(homosexual).*

As a result, there are four population subgroups, as shown in Figure 1.2; male heterosexuals, male homosexuals, female heterosexuals, and female homosexuals.

Our analysis will be restricted to *heterosexual* males and females, for several reasons. Firstly, a meaningful comparison of heterosexuals with homosexuals requires a completely separate analysis, as extensive as this one devoted to differences between heterosexual males and females.

Secondly, the most productive analysis of homosexuality does not center on a comparison of *males* and *females,* as in our analysis. Rather, the comparison of most interest is in the

Gender

		Female	Male
Sexual Affinity	*Female*	Female Homosexual	Male Heterosexual
	Male	Female Heterosexual	Male Homosexual

Figure 1.2—The *gender* × *sexual affinity* matrix, and the resultant four population subgroups.

differences between male homosexuals and male heterosexuals, and between female homosexuals and female heterosexuals.

Thirdly, heterosexuals comprise approximately 90% of the population—by most estimates—which is enough for any theory to encompass, without unduly complicating it for an additional 10% of the population.

However, it must be noted from the start that any analysis of heterosexual gender dynamics is made more difficult by the fact that many homosexuals remain *covert*. Thus for valid observations, it is necessary to sort through *four different types* of male-female interaction: (1) male *heterosexual* with female *heterosexual*, (2) male *heterosexual* with female *homosexual*, (3) male *homosexual* with female *heterosexual*, and (4) male *homosexual* with female *homosexual*. The present analysis is restricted to the first alternative, not out of insensitivity to homosexuals, but as a pragmatic matter, with full recognition that life is not so simple as boys chasing girls; but it is the major part.

So, throughout our comparison of males and females it should be kept in mind that we are excluding homosexuals from our analysis, so that we need not repeatedly qualify our gender generalizations, which in most cases do not apply to homosexuals. The discussion of homosexual behavior will be introduced only on a few occasions where it will provide extra insight into the basic differences between males and females in the predominantly heterosexual population.

5. Universal vs. Cultural Differences

In our study of behavioral gender differences we will concentrate on universal broad-based differences rather than on unique local cultural differences. More specifically, we will look at males and females in contemporary Western civilization, as represented most notably in America and Europe. Local cultural variations in gender behavior will only be of interest in that they demonstrate the same dynamics seen in contemporary Western society, or exhibit the earlier stages of modern behavior.

This particular bias is based on the observation that the media-dominant American and European cultures play a leadership role in the evolution of behavioral patterns around the world.

Also, our search is not for superficial local differences in male and female behavior in isolated regions of Borneo or the Amazon basin, or even in a small community in Montana, or what may have been the norm centuries ago. Rather, we are interested in the latest form of gender behavior, which can be interpreted as universal in nature, with special emphasis on the *evolutionary dynamics* of the behavior.

The behavioral characteristics of bygone eras, or isolated geographic areas, or ritualized cultures, are of only secondary interest; with the assumption that they, too, with time, will succumb to the gender dynamics observed in the cutting edge of contemporary Western culture, if they do not already conform to it either in detail or in principle.

We emphasize this aspect of our analysis now, so that we do not have to repeatedly interrupt our presentation to qualify our generalizations with the fact that an exception exists in a remote region of the Himalayas. There are cultures that have not yet invented the wheel, but that does not invalidate an analysis of the automobile, or the physics of angular motion. Our primary interest, then, is in modern Western culture.

6. The Importance of Grooming Behavior

Until now we have spoken in the abstract about behavioral differences between males and females without having specified our area of interest. As noted at the start, while most individuals acknowledge biological differences between males and females, a large contingent of scholars deny that significant behavioral differences also exist.

Consequently, in order to document behavioral gender differences to the satisfaction of all, we must identify behaviors for which males and females differ so dramatically that there can be no doubt to their existence. Only then can we use that data as support for a theory of gender dynamics, for a theory is only as strong as the extent of phenomenon that it explains.

With these requirements in mind we have chosen to study gender differences in *grooming behavior;* specifically, hair grooming, cosmetics usage, jewelry wearing, and clothing preferences. These are clearly observable forms of behavior and do not require complicated measuring operations that are subject to dispute; unlike the documentation of abstract behavioral complexes such as intelligence, nurturance, relational need, affect, or moral development, which no one can unambiguously define, much less reliably measure.

Grooming behavior, on the other hand, in addition to being easily observed and measured, is, on face value alone, intimately related to gender *mating dynamics,* perhaps the most important of all types of behavior.

Another advantage of studying grooming behavior is that it provides multiple reliability checks for any conclusions we may draw with respect to gender differences. Firstly, there are the four broad and presumably independent behavioral areas of *hair grooming, cosmetics usage, jewelry wearing,* and *clothing preferences.* Secondly, within each of these broad categories of conduct there are dozens upon dozens of individual behaviors. Consequently, if we see the same gender differences *within,* as well as *between* behavioral categories, we will have amassed an overwhelming set of data in support of male and female behavioral differences.

If we can then present a theory that integrates this mass of data, consistent with the basic reproductive roles of males and females, with clear implications for societal policy decisions and changes, which address the ills of contemporary civilization, and motivate others to act on these conclusions, then we will have accomplished our goals. Our plate is full, so let us begin.

Chapter 2

Hair Grooming

1. Introduction

When we think of *hair* we typically think of the hair on the tops of our heads. And yet, our entire bodies are literally covered with hair. In addition to the hair on the tops of our heads, we have significant amounts of hair on our faces, our arms, our underarms, our chests, our legs, and our genital areas.

It should be no surprise, then, that our hair plays a very central role in our lives, although it may not be realized at first glance just how important it is. Males differ among themselves in the quantity and nature of the hair on their bodies, as do females. Although we will be interested in gender differences in head and body hair, our primary concern will be how males and females differ in the treatment of their hair.

Perhaps more than any other discriminating variable that we study, hair grooming behavior will provide us with the greatest insights into the basic differences between males and females.

2. Head Hair

To begin our study of gender differences in hair grooming, let us start at the very top, with the hair on the tops of our heads.

By analyzing the ways in which males and females differ in their behavior toward their head hair, we will begin to understand that there are some fundamental behavioral differences between males and females that go well beyond the primary biological differences noted in the opening chapter.

Length. Since we were young, we learned that girls have long hair and boys have short hair. I can still remember the moment, when as a child, I asked my parents why girls had long hair and boys had short hair. They looked at me sideways, and then at one another through squinted eyes, as if their suspicions had been confirmed that they had indeed raised an imbecile.

Many years and much schooling later, I still had not received an answer to that apparently simple question about gender differences in hair length. It was this issue of hair length, more than anything else, that led me to a closer analysis of the basic differences between males and females.

Even a casual observation of males and females will prove that females have longer hair on their heads than males. Not only is the *average* length of hair greater for females than males, but the *variation* in the length of hair is also greater for females. That is, female head hair ranges from very short—occasionally as short as the shortest man's—to very long; while males generally have close-cropped hair, with exceptionally long male hair being the exception.

So, there are clear-cut gender differences both in average hair length and variation in hair length; *with extremely wide variation among females in their hair length, while there is minimal variation in hair length among males.* This gender difference results in a *homogenization* of males. That is, it tends to make males more alike to one another. The longer hair of females, and the wide variation in length, on the other hand, tends to *maximize the differences* among females. We will see that this type of behavior—which minimizes differences among males, while maximizing differences among females—will appear over and over again as we study other types of behavior which discriminate males and females.

Since this difference in hair length between males and females begins in infancy, one possible explanation for its pervasiveness is that it begins as a behavioral method for telling infant boys and girls apart, and that this hair grooming behavior persists through old age. While on the surface this seems a plausible explanation, there is much that follows that argues against it. Although the gender of some infants is difficult to discern, by and large it is pretty easy to discriminate a boy from a girl based on facial and skeletal features and bodily movements. Such dramatic differences in hair length are not needed to tell boys from girls. Also, in later sections we will analyze other behavior directed toward head hair which differs drastically between males and females, and pretty much destroys the theory that hair length is necessary to discriminate boys from girls, with the implicit assumption that they need to be differentiated from one another in the first place.

The common *feminist* explanation for the longer hair of females, and the wider variation among them in its length, vis-à-vis males, is that this hair growing behavior is forced upon them by a male-dominated society conspiring against their happiness. Because men are in a position of power, they have the ability to crop their hair close to the head, minimizing differences among themselves, reducing their hair care labor, while *women are forced to grow their hair long and of widely varying length,* creating an imposition on their free time. We will examine the plausibility of this explanation later, when we consider other differences between males and females in their hair grooming behavior.

For now, we can gain some insight into the gender differences in hair length by studying recent historical events. Prior to the 1960's, the variation in hair length among males was virtually zero, with every male sporting hair cropped close to the skull at the sides, with a few inches at most on the top, with even shorter flat-top styles also in popularity. Then in the Sixties, there was a sudden change in male hair length among a portion of the male population. This change coincided with a confluence of events which were seen to be responsible for an expansion of individual and societal consciousness, not the least of these events being the introduction of marijuana and psychedelic products into the youth culture; the effect of these products seeming to supplant cortical behavioral control with the more primitive subcortical brain functions which are less prone to learning effects.

This sudden change in male hair growth, from flat-top crewcut to shaggy moptop, underscored the awareness and possibility that gender differences in hair length *were not written into our genetic code*—etched in stone, as it were—but rather were arbitrary standards imposed by cultural forces. But within a decade, only rock musicians retained long hair, while the majority of the male population returned to the close-cropped standard that existed prior to the Sixties. This behavioral resilience of male hair length, bouncing back to its previous standard within a decade, suggests strong forces at work— whether a kind of biological or cultural primacy—and hints that perhaps the long-standing and intransigent female behavior of wearing their hair longer than males has a very fundamental cause and is not entirely arbitrary.

Were hair length the only behavioral difference between males and females, it could easily be dismissed as a curiosity with little real importance. But as we consider other hair-related behavior, we will begin to suspect that differences in hair grooming habits among males and females have much more importance than we ever realized.

Styling. Not only do males and females differ in the average length of their hair and their variation in hair length, but they also differ significantly in the *styling* of their hair. To some extent the gender difference in hair styling is dependent upon the previously documented difference in hair length. There are certain things you can do with twelve inches of hair that you cannot do with two inches of hair. Still, notwithstanding this potential for greater variation in female hair styling, based on their longer hair, we observe that even without this ingoing bias, females vary in their hair styling significantly more than males.

One way to make this additional gender difference in hair styling perfectly clear, and to separate it as being distinct from the hair length difference, is to compare a sample of men and women with hair of *equal length*. In this way we can see that variation between males and females in hair styling is independent of their overall differences in hair length. Although there are relatively few females with hair cropped to the head, and still fewer males with hair to the small of their back, there are subpopulations of males and females with hair of equal length. These are the groups we should compare to gain insight into gender differences in hair styling, as separate from the observed differences in hair length alone.

When we compare a random sample of females with, say, five inches of hair, with a sample of males with equally long hair, the gender difference in hair styling is dramatic and undeniable. In comparison to the females, the males are once again relatively *homogeneous* in their hair styling, while in contrast the females style their hair to *maximize differences* among themselves. They may cut their hair on the skew; they may or may not have "bangs" of varying length; they may layer cut it; they may braid it, once, twice, or many times; they may gather it in a pony tail at the back, right-side, left-side, right- *and* left-side, or at the top of the head; they may adorn it with a ribbon or barrette; they may curl or straighten it; they may spray it with grooming substances; and they may color it. I, myself, have a particular weakness for girls who wear a pony tail, especially those that sprout from the top of the head, perhaps with a colorful ribbon, so I know that these things actually do work.

Now there will always be that philosopher who dismisses the above generalizations about gender differences in hair styling by recalling an instance or two where a male had been seen to exhibit all of the above hair styling behaviors, as if the exception in human affairs disproves the rule, rather than proving it. But anyone with eyes to see will agree that there are clearcut gender differences in hair *styling* behavior, quite independent of differences in hair *length*.

While more anecdotal in nature, one final observation about gender hair length is worth noting. Very often, when a girl more or less demurely deflates the bravado of a courting male, which they are wont to do, the humbled young man is often seen the next day with his tail between his legs and his hair shorn close to the skull. This dynamic is supported metaphorically by the biblical tale of how Samson lost his hair and power to Delilah's scissors.

The "part." There is one particular piece of hair styling behavior, more than any other, that provides insight into the fundamental difference between males and females in their grooming behavior, and that is the use of the "part," the way in which the hair on the top of the head is divided with a comb so as to flow in opposite directions.

Without yet understanding why, we have already seen many times how female hair grooming behavior is aimed at maximizing differences among themselves, while males act to minimize differences among themselves. Now, with the use of the "part" the above gender dynamics are put in even clearer relief.

Whether one looks at the males in their daily life or those appearing on TV or in magazines, one cannot help but observe that the vast majority of males—perhaps more than 90%—part their hair in *exactly the same spot* on the side of their heads. Not only is it remarkable that so many males part their hair on the side of their heads, but what is most amazing is the lack of variation in exactly where it is located. If one were to measure it, the standard "part" would be found to be located approximately 45° from the vertical axis of the head, rotating from a point directly between the eyes.

One cannot help but be impressed with this uniformity in male hair grooming. To make it even more interesting is the fact that the part is usually on the *left* side of the head, perhaps as much as in 90% of the cases. Never mind for the moment why males part their hair on the side of the head, why don't they split 50:50 in their choice of *which side* of the head they place their part. At least this question has a relatively simple answer. Since most males are right-handed (generally agreed to be a genetic factor) their combing behavior makes a part on the left side of the head more manageable, and further shows us how behavior is dictated by genetics.

What is more difficult to answer is why *males* choose to part their hair at the side of the head, while *females* tend to part theirs in the middle of the head, or not all. Even among females who do part their hair on the side of the head, the location of the part varies in degree from the vertical axis of the head, rather than being ritualized in exactly the same spot as it is among males.

So here, once again, we see the gender dynamic which results in a *homogenization of males,* while *maximizing differences among females.* The explanation of my *feminist* friends for this wide variation in hair-parting behavior among females, in contrast to that of males, is that they are victims of *male cultural hegemony.* Were it not for the fact that males have all the power in society, the feminists believe that they too could part their hair in a uniform location on the side of the head. This same explanation was forwarded for the wide variation in hair length and styling among females, and we may have to delve deeper into gender differences before we can assess the plausibility of this feminist explanation.

Perhaps the most likely theory explaining the ritualized male hair-parting behavior is based on the generally negative female view of bald men. Why else would so many balding males resort to the transparent and sometimes ridiculous behavior of growing the remaining hair on the side of the head to exaggerated lengths in order to throw it over the top of their bald pate, leaving the now less mysterious part on the side of the head.

One can speculate that the wives of these men then proceeded to comb the hair of their male children "just like daddy." This is the evolutionary course that much ingrained behavior has followed. It begins as *functional* behavior, moves on to *stylized* variations, and finally becomes *ritualized* to the point that its origins have been lost. As we study other forms of behavior that seem to have been cast in stone, we will observe this same *fuction-style-ritual* sequence in its development. Since such ritualized behavior has usually persisted beyond its functional origins, it is important to recognize such behaviors wherever they might exist, and, if appropriate, break free from them. The comical "part" can serve as a constant reminder of just how much of our behavior is shaped by unconscious forces.

Since our primary concern here is with gender dynamics, we should now consider the role that females play in the male hair-parting behavior. As already observed, the balding male resorts to parting his hair at the side in order to cover his natural hair loss. Or, he may resort to sporting a wig, which, most interestingly, usually has the ritual part at the side. Although some of this behavior might be ascribed to the personal vanity of trying to retain the characteristics of one's youth, it most surely has a female component, to the extent that females discriminate among balding men in their words and actions.

It seems that only monks, Yul Brynner types, political leaders, artists, babies, and occasional eccentrics are comfortable with a bald head. My advice to other balding men, as I am among them, is to shave off *all* their hair, for every method of concealment is laughably transparent, and retaining a rim of hair around the side of the head only serves to *highlight* the baldness. In contrast, a fully shaven head avoids the schizo-phrenic balding dome with its highly contrasting hairy rim, all of which only serves to distract from other facial features. Now that I remove all the hair from my head, I am even more hand-some than I was when I was in high school and had a full head of hair; but in a different sort of way, if you know what I mean.

Perhaps it is not entirely coincidental that baldness is a ge-netic trait restricted to males (and babies). The stereotype that baldness is not as desirable as a full head of hair, is further evidence that hair does in fact play a very important role in gender dynamics. But since baldness is a biological phenome-non, and our prime interest is in behavior, we will not specu-late any further into the reasons why males have this trait and females do not, and why the trait engenders diffidence among a sizable portion of men, as evidenced by their efforts to conceal it.

We stated at the start we would exclude the *homosexual* population from our analysis, unless it offered the opportunity for further understanding of gender dynamics among the het-erosexual population. In this context, a worthwhile area of re-search would be to compare heterosexual and homosexual males with respect to their attitudes toward, incidence of, and reactions to, baldness. If homosexuals are more sensitive to baldness than heterosexuals, and are more likely to attempt concealment, and differ from heterosexual males in other ways, especially their relations with women, it could account in part for the development of societal stereotypes and *negative female attitudes* toward balding men, especially those who try trans-parent and often laughable methods of concealment.

To combat negative stereotypes, I am urging a new breed of balding men to shave or shear off *all* their hair, and notice how much better the skinhead-look fares in comparison to the traditional rimmed look, or concealment tactic. It is the only way to escape a stereotype that might have some basis in reality. And a final word to those who give baldness a bad image and insist on trying to conceal it: whomever you are trying to fool, *it isn't working.*

While the genetic and evolutionary aspects of male baldness are intriguing topics of study, for our purposes it is enough to recognize that *biological baldness* probably accounted for the *ritualized hair-parting behavior* observed in the male population. Also important from the gender dynamics viewpoint is that females play a role both in attitudes toward male baldness and in perpetuating the ritualized male hair-parting behavior through their grooming of their children's hair in the image of their fathers.

Up to this point we have observed blatant gender differences in hair length, hair styling, and the use of the hair "part." Next we will build upon this foundation of differences as we consider yet other differences between males and females in the way they behave toward the hair on their heads.

Curling, straightening, and crimping. Another major difference between males and females involves the extent to which they curl, straighten, or crimp their hair. There can be little argument that females engage in these hair grooming behaviors considerably more often than males. Although an occasional male may have a supply of hair curlers, many more females use them or regularly visit beauty parlors to have them attached to their hair to produce curls. Yet other females will crimp their hair with custom tools that produce a ripple pattern. All of this is usually topped off with a hair spray to keep everything in place.

This widespread hair-curling behavior among females of all ages suggests that natural curliness is something to be imitated.

Elderly women are especially fond of visiting the beauty parlor on a regular basis to have their hair curled. There may be something intrinsically more appealing about curls than limp hair, although we have all seen attractive women with both types of hair style.

But arguing against the interpretation that curly hair is intrinsically attractive is the desire among many females to straighten their hair, whether through a hot iron or relaxing substances. In contrast, relatively few males engage in this type of hair curling and straightening behavior.

The expected explanation of my feminist friends for this uniquely female behavior is that they are trapped in a society in which males have all the power, and that they are being forced in subtle ways to engage in this hair curling, hair crimping, and hair straightening behavior, just as they are forced to wear their hair at extreme lengths. Now although this explanation may be valid, it seems too simplistic, unimaginative, incoherent, and all-encompassing in its nature, and provides little insight into the evolutionary and volitional dynamics of the behavior, so we must try to uncover other explanations that account for these great behavioral differences between males and females of the human species.

Hair coloring. Very often we can judge the extent of a particular type of behavior by the monetary value of the product market it engenders. With this criterion alone, we are forced to acknowledge that the coloring of hair is a highly popular activity. It, like other hair grooming practices, constitutes a gigantic consumer market.

And here again, we observe gender differences. While many males will use dyes to cover their graying hair, females in much greater numbers, and of all ages, are interested in changing the color of their hair, whether gray or not.

The covering of graying hair is obviously an attempt to retain the qualities of youth, of which few individuals are emotionally prepared to let go. Here again, aside from personal vanities, gender dynamics play a prime motivating factor in the determination of the hair coloring behavior. Whether in fact, or in imagination, many graying individuals believe that they will have higher worth in the eyes of their peers and the other gender if they conceal the graying of their hair.

Graying hair is a biological process of aging, much like baldness (but impartial to gender), and so it has similar negative connotations in a society placing a premium on some of the more superficial qualities of youth. But in fact, graying hair also has much positive significance, in that it is often a sign of *sophistication, wisdom,* and *leadership,* whether among legislators, educators, scientists, or captains of industry. Notice the ritual white wigs often worn by judges and legislators. Also, one cannot help but note that in gorilla societies, the *old silverback* is revered and regularly approached unhesitatingly by *adolescent females* for his attention. Still, among modern males in the human species, there are those who consider silver hair a liability rather than an asset.

Whatever the reasons for males coloring their gray hair, feminists argue that since they are deprived of positions of power in the august professions, their gray hair is of little value and so they are forced to color it, much as they are forced by the male-dominated society to grow their hair long and subject it to all manner of styling variations.

But curiously, it is not just gray-haired females who resort to coloring their hair. Many females still in their teens, twenties, thirties, or forties will change their hair from brunette to blond or choose to be redheads or perhaps various shades of these basic hair colors. Why young females engage in this activity, and young males do not, is certainly a valid question to ponder.

Even at this early stage of analysis, we suspect that this hair coloring behavior among females reflects a basic gender difference, and that it is inextricably intermeshed with the other hair grooming behaviors discussed above, where it was observed that females grow their hair to long and varying lengths and groom it in distinctive ways with the end result being a *maximization of the differences among themselves:* this in contrast to male hair grooming behavior, which tends to *minimize their differences.*

Although we still have many other types of hair grooming behavior to analyze, the gender differences uncovered to this point, in which females act to maximize the differences among themselves, suggests that they are *competing with one another for a limited number of desirable males.* This is consistent with the often-heard female complaint that a good man is hard to find.

In turn, this suggests that the distribution of favorable qualities in the male population is highly skewed vis-à-vis that of the female population. Such a basic difference in the *composition* of the male and female populations has extremely far-reaching implications, and we will keep an eye on this hypothesis as we expand our analysis of gender differences in behavior.

Until now, we have only compared males and females with respect to the hair on the top of the head, but with interesting results. We will now look at the ways in which females and males differ in the treatment of their *facial hair* to see if we can gain any further support for our conclusions to this point.

3. Eyebrows

We have observed dramatic differences between males and females with respect to the ways in which they behave toward the hair on the *top* of the head. If this were the total extent of gender differences in hair grooming, it would be eye-opening in itself, but there are still further differences that we can analyze, many of which center on *facial* hair. We can begin our study of facial hair with an examination of the *eyebrows,* those curious patches of hair above our eyes; which, incidentally, usually retain their natural color long after the rest of our hair has turned white.

Before we consider gender differences in eyebrow grooming, it is worthwhile to speculate on their evolutionary development and importance. The movement of the muscles in the forehead and above the eyes are correlated with all manner of emotions, including, but not limited to, amazement, anxiety, fear, doubt, consternation, stress, joy, worry, and surprise, to name a few.

For example, when you suddenly see someone you recognize or are attracted to, your eyebrows reflexively rise, saying more to the other person than words could ever communicate. Similarly, other emotions are correlated with their own peculiar eyebrow motions, angles, and slants, serving a strong and reliable communications function. What our tongues conceal, our brows reveal.

If we had hair all over our faces, like certain primates, the movements of the brows would not be so noticeable, especially at a distance. But with just a sliver or patch of eyebrow hair, the movements are easily discernible, and nonverbal communication with others—the most genuine, valid, and undisguisable kind—is greatly facilitated. Given this very important communication function, the eyebrows were destined to evolve in stylized directions. With this as background, let us consider the ways in which we humans treat our eyebrows.

If you look at the individuals you meet in your daily life, or those appearing in the media, you will discover that a person's eyebrows are very much a personal signature. They differ dramatically on a wide variety of dimensions, including color, location relative to the eyes, thickness, horizontal and vertical width, texture, and perhaps most interestingly, the particular arch or curvature that they follow.

The above half dozen or so dimensions on which eyebrows differ generate a vast number of different possible combinations. Even if we admit only *two* possible values for each of *six* eyebrow variables, there are $2\times2\times2\times2\times2\times2 = 64$ possible composites. If we admit *three* levels of each variable, there are $3^6 = 729$ possible combinations. But, since in fact there are more than six eyebrow variables to consider and more than three levels of each of the variables, the actual number of eyebrow types is in the *thousands*. Indeed, there are probably more types of eyebrows than there are styles of hair on the tops of our heads, or even the types of noses, chins, or mouths.

With so many different types of eyebrows it follows that some types are inherently more attractive than others, and it will be noticed that they are usually a signature characteristic of *icons of beauty*. Many females recognize this fact and engage in behavior to modify their eyebrows to mimic those which they find intrinsically more appealing. This is accomplished in two basic ways. Firstly, they will use tweezers or other instruments to pluck hairs from eyebrows in order to modify them in any number of respects, whether thickness, horizontal or vertical width, or curvature and arch. Secondly, they will use colored pencils to finish the job, by coloring in the desired eyebrow outline. The color choice may or may not match the original eyebrow color, depending upon personal aesthetic judgments.

While there is no objective measure of exactly what percentage of the female population alters their eyebrows in such a manner, the size of the cosmetics market for eyebrow-enhancing products is substantial, and casual observation of the female population suggests that this type of grooming behavior is very widespread.

The percentage of the male population that plucks its eyebrows or uses colored pencils or dyes to enhance their natural eyebrows is relatively small. So, by inspection of the male and female populations we can safely assert that there does in fact exist a gender difference in eyebrow grooming behavior.

The end result again, is a *maximization of differences* among females vis-à-vis males. This is based on the reasonable assumption that those females who do alter their eyebrows, are changing from common or "average" eyebrows in order to produce new ones which are relatively rare in their natural form. This behavioral pattern of imitating rare, intrinsically appealing features, has already been observed among females with respect to their dying, bleaching, and curling of head hair.

So, the number of gender differences we have uncovered continues to grow, and so far we have only considered a fraction of all hair grooming habits; having not yet moved beneath the neck, for we still have more facial hair to consider.

4. Eyelashes

Just below the eyebrows are the *eyelashes*. Although eyelashes do not differ so much as eyebrows, they still vary considerable from one individual to another. Perhaps the most important variables upon which eyelashes differ include color, density (or spacing between lashes), length, and their curvature. Still, this leaves a lot to work with for those interested in improving upon what they were born with, and the cosmetics industry provides a vast variety of products to accomplish the task.

A product called *mascara,* and an accompanying application brush, is an all-purpose and extremely popular means of enhancing the eyelashes, for in a single stroke the *color, texture, density,* and *length* of the eyelashes can be altered from their natural state. Again, the behavior is aimed at emulating lashes which are considered to be intrinsically attractive.

In addition, there is a kind of *hemostat-like* instrument which is used to clamp and curl the eyelashes. This operation prior to the application of the mascara yields eyelashes that are long, lush, and attractively curved. When all else fails, there are *false eyelashes* which can be glued onto the eyelids.

By and large the use of mascara, curling tools, and prosthetics on the eyelashes is limited to the *female* population, and I think few will deny this. The end result, again, is to increase the *differences* among females. Common ordinary looking eyelashes decrease in number, and relatively rare outstanding lashes increase in number. As more females with commonplace lashes come closer to looking like females with naturally attractive lashes, these latter females adopt the mascara habit themselves in order to keep a step ahead of their competitive sisters and female peers.

We have now considered gender differences with respect to the hair on the top of the head and the hair around the eyes, and have discovered that there are blatant differences between males and females with respect to the ways in which they groom this hair. Our observations show that females act to *maximize* the differences among themselves, while males act to *minimize* their differences. We have theorized that these asymmetric gender differences are motivated by a drive among females to compete for the attentions of a relatively small number of desirable males. Note how frequently females cut their long hair soon after marriage.

If it is true that this female behavior, which maximizes the differences among themselves—usually by imitating instances of rarer, naturally occurring beauty—is reflecting an *underlying competition for a limited number of desirable males,* we are forced to further hypothesize the radical notion that *polygamy* is the natural order among humans as it is in most of the animal kingdom, wherein a relatively small number of the male population—the most desirable—mate with a number of females, ensuring the optimum quality of the succeeding generation. At this point it is too soon to develop this multi-faceted proposition in greater detail, until we have marshalled further evidence in its favor.

We still have many other gender differences to analyze with respect to hair grooming, to see if they exist and whether they support the above theory. We are optimistic that a further analysis of hair grooming habits will support our theory of gender dynamics, since we have already learned so much simply by looking at the *hair on the tops our head,* and at the *hair around our eyes.*

5. The Beard

We are now ready to examine the *beard,* the facial hair covering the cheeks and chins of members of the post-pubescent male population. Since this facial hair is largely restricted to adult males, an assessment of gender differences with respect to its grooming is not totally comparable to the other types of analysis that we have performed so far, in which males and females were on equal footing with respect to their hair availability.

Still, an analysis of how males behave toward their beards, and female attitudes and behavior toward male beards, will further our basic understanding of gender dynamics.

Although an interesting topic, it is not our primary purpose to decide why males have beards while females do not. It is a biological reality, and our prime interest is with the behavior related to this biology.

Just as there are thousands of types of eyebrows and hair styles, there must be an equal number of types of beards, varying in color, texture, thickness, and contour. What is most interesting from the very start is the fact that much of the contemporary male population has *eliminated* their beards, thereby removing another major male distinguishing characteristic, producing even greater *homogeneity* among males than that created by the cropping of the hair on their heads.

Indeed, a sizable portion of the male population has lived their *entire lives* without ever having seen the beard with which they were born, having shaved it from puberty to the grave. Why would men shave their beards and not the hair off the top of their heads? Although we consider a number of explanations below, we cannot escape the conclusion that the beard removal behavior has the dual effect of making males more similar to one another, and more similar to females in appearance. We should keep these end results in mind as we try to determine the origins and reasons for the beard shaving behavior, for behavior is often best understood in terms of its consequences rather than in the actions themselves.

It is safe to assume that at one time all men wore beards. And just as head hair and eyebrows differ in their intrinsic attractiveness, it is safe to assume that some natural beards were more aesthetically pleasing than others, as measured by, say, their attractiveness to females. Who has not seen sculptures or movies of the Greek and Roman Empires where the heroes had more attractive beards than the common men. It would be no surprise, then, if men with commonplace beards did not try to emulate the attractive ones by trimming it here and there, to match the contours of the aesthetic natural beards, just as females groom their hair, eyebrows, and eyelashes to emulate natural beauty.

Although this explains beard grooming, it does not explain why the beard should have virtually disappeared in modern times. Indeed, the demise of the beard is so widespread that the presence of a beard is considered by many as an *unnatural* state. Anyone who has allowed his beard to grow will be familiar with the common questions, "Why are you growing a beard?" or "How come you have a beard?" as if the clean-shaven face were the *natural* order.

Somewhere in history, someone shaved his beard and the behavior caught on with the entire male population. It is interesting to note that the exceptions to the shaving behavior are concentrated among religious figures or groups, who consider shaving one's natural hair an unnatural abomination, and yet many of these same religions require the surgical removal of an infant male's *penis foreskin*, which is among the most important and functional of all anatomical and physiological characteristics, certainly not comparable to hair.

As for facial hair, there are a number of possible explanations of why shaving caught the imagination of the male population, and probably no one reason is totally adequate. Rather, it may have been the combination of a number of factors, some of which we will consider, always with an eye toward the role played by females of the species, since our primary interest is in gender dynamics.

We have already observed that society places a premium on youthful features. Also, we have noted that the coloring of graying hair is a common practice among both males and females. It is safe to assume, then, that the appearance of gray hair is a source of anxiety among a sizable portion of the population. We can speculate, then, that the once virile male sporting a handsome beard might become a bit apprehensive about the turning of his beard to gray, which often happens well before the hair on the top of the head turns gray. Everyone has seen graybeards with dark hair. If the anxiety about losing one's youthful features is accompanied by a real or imagined diminution of female attention, the graybearded males might be tempted to successively trim the graying areas until the entire beard is gone. If this is accompanied by a real or imagined increase in female attention, the beard shaving habit would be reinforced and others would imitate this successful ploy.

We have noted how balding men use the tactic of parting their hair on the side, and sweeping it over their bald pate; speculating that mothers then perpetuated this "part" by employing it on their sons so that they looked like their fathers. Similarly, it could well be that clean-shaven fathers serve as role models for their sons, who perpetuate the behavior to the next generation.

The face shaving behavior may also have started with male homosexuals, as they distanced themselves from the typical male look and more closely approximated the female face. (But then this raises the question as to exactly which male characteristics turn on the homosexual.) It is also possible that some males shaved their beards in deference to preferences of their lesbian mates.

Another possibility for the start of the shaving habit is that males with scraggly or puny beards, unable to compete with the more stalwart models sported by the men most in favor among the young maidens, reacted by shaving their faces clean of their sparse and pathetic beard. If this enhanced their stature among females, from what it had been, the shaving behavior would no doubt spread among other males.

Still another possibility, germaine to our analysis, is that females may have found kissing a shaven man something of a novelty and less damaging to their valued complexion. This is unlikely to be the sole cause of male shaving behavior, but we have learned that most behavior has *multiple causes* which combine in additive or more complex ways to produce the end product. What is most interesting for our analysis is how male shaving behavior is determined to a large extent by female behavior, an indirect precursor of male vanity.

Since young yet virile boys are often devoid of a beard, the adult male who shaves his face may do so to acquire a new youthful image, even if his beard has not yet turned gray. If this increases his stature among young females, the shaving behavior will no doubt be imitated by others.

The profile of one's jawbones and chin, and the location of the mouth relative to them, are very important determinants of intrinsic facial appeal. For those with exceptionally handsome facial features, the beard that conceals them can be a liability, unless it is equally exceptional. The removal of the beard to reveal these attractive facial features was no doubt another source of the shaving phenomenon.

Finally, in addition to all of the above possible causes, and many that have probably escaped us, we must consider the contribution of modern technology and commerce, wherein sharp razors, and eventually electric razors, were marketed to the male population. Among men, gadgets have a validity of their own.

An analysis of beard dynamics would not be complete without a consideration of the *moustache* and *sideburns.* The moustache can take on almost as many forms as the eyebrows, and perhaps because of this, many males groom the hair above their upper lips much like females groom their eyebrows. Notice how the moustache, along with the two eyebrows, completes an aesthetic triangle on the face.

The moustache has come to be much more popular than the full beard, the natural endowment of males, so we are likely to learn something from an analysis of this attempt to improve upon nature. A moustache on a man can look anywhere from dashing to ridiculous, but since there is no accounting for taste, each style has its own following.

As to why the moustache caught on as an alternative to the full beard or a fully shaven face is anyone's guess. Certainly the first man who shaved off his full beard enjoyed the attention of his peers when it was first done, and as already observed, the novelty of this clean-shaven face must have met with approval by the females of his attention, perpetuating the behavior. In contrast, the first man who shaved his beard, leaving only the patch of hair above his upper lip, must have been met with hilarious laughter, even so sometimes today. Indeed, one theory of the origin of the "moustache" name is that the very first moustached man was greeted by certain of his cruelest peers with, "Yo! What's that *mouse* under your nose!"

Still, one cannot deny that that touch of hair above the lip does add a certain character—be it positive or negative—to the male who sports it, much as a person's eyebrows are a personal signature. The same can be said for sideburns, the remnants of the beard next to the ears. Also, we cannot deny that many movie stars, occupying the status of sex symbol, also wear a moustache or sideburns. A man's moustache may also be imitated by his son, perpetuating the behavior into the next generation. Fathers and sons with matching moustaches are so common that one would think that the principles of biological inheritance were at work.

Although one association of the moustache is with the swashbuckling Hollywood hero, another is with the man who has grown bald, and wears the moustache, it seems, as a compensation or counterbalance for the hair lost on the top of the head. This combination of the bald head and a moustache is so common that it is probably similar in its dynamic to the balding man who sweeps the overgrown hair at the side of his head over the top of the head. We have speculated that this was the origin of the ritual "part" as mothers groomed their sons to look like their fathers. Similarly, the moustache may have begun with a balding man trying to hang on to what seemed to him to be a slipping away of his youthful appearance and his diminished attraction to desirable females.

In this context, it is worthwhile to note that a *full beard* on a balding man is a much more effective foil to the bald head than the moustache. The beard forms a continuous flow with the remaining hair on the sides of the head, while the moustache only serves to highlight the islands of hair above the ears, creating a very cluttered look, wherein the moustache and islands of hair on the side of the head compete with the eyebrows for attention. For example, see Figure 2.1 for various male hair grooming patterns.

Whatever the reasons, the moustache has taken on a reality of its own, as if it were a natural anatomical feature written in the genetic code, while the full beard, which is in fact written

Figure 2.1—Different types of male hair grooming patterns.

in the genes, is considered unnatural. Here we see the dynamics of behavioral evolution in its clearest relief. When we see how easily such behavioral features can evolve from one generation to another—usually by virtue of their contribution to an enhanced mating potential—it is not hard to understand how anatomical and physiological characteristics could evolve over the millennia by similar dynamics.

In summary, although the facial beard is a uniquely male characteristic, we have found that female attitudes and behavior play a central role in the motivation of male beard grooming behavior.

We have now analyzed the hair on the tops of our heads, as well as our eyebrows, eyelashes, beards, moustaches, and sideburns. We have skipped over the discussion of the hair spilling out of our nostrils, or growing on the tip our nose, only because we can agree among ourselves that there is little to be learned in this area with regard to gender differences, for we can agree from the start that few individuals, male or female, consider *nose hair* a really attractive feature. Similarly for hair sprouting out of our ears.

6. Head Hair Reviewed

To this point we have only analyzed the hair on our body from the neck up, without yet having considered the hair on the rest of the body. To summarize our findings so far, we have found that there are dramatic gender differences with regard to the grooming of head hair, and that these differences between males and females follow a systematic and meaningful pattern.

The most striking differences uncovered between males and females with respect to the grooming of head hair include (1) the longer average hair length among females, (2) a greater variation in hair styling among females, (3) a greater incidence of hair coloring among females, and (4) an almost exclusively female effort to enhance their eyebrows and eyelashes. In addition, we found that the exclusively male grooming habits surrounding baldness and the facial beard may be dictated to a large extent by female attitudes and behavior.

Taken together, these gender differences reveal that females consistently act in ways to *maximize the differences* among themselves, while males *minimize their differences*. These dramatic differences between male and female hair grooming behaviors were interpreted to signify an underlying *competition among females* to attract the attention of *a limited number of desirable males*. This female competition for a scarcity of prime males, in turn supports the theory that the composition of the human population is such that *polygamy* is the natural biological drive among humans as it is in most animal species, wherein the most capable males have the highest probability of mating with multiple female partners, with the positive result that the succeeding generations are slanted toward their desirable characteristics.

That this analysis is far afield from contemporary mainstream thought is evidenced by a lack of scholarly appreciation for the supporting data itself, much less the theory; as proven by a recent American space probe (Pioneer 10) which included a plaque containing a frontal view of a nude male and female standing side by side, aimed at communicating with other worlds about Earth's most intelligent species. The male and female shown on this interstellar postcard differ in a number of important respects: namely, the female has *long hair*, while the male has *short hair;* the male has *no beard;* and yes, the male has a ritual "part" located on the left side of his head, 45° from the vertical!

Now if our interstellar neighbors are in possession of our genome by some means, which they most assuredly are (if only based on the number of alien abductions reported in the tabloid press), they may well be perplexed why that plaque—produced with the assistance of leading scientists from our most elite universities—shows males and females with characteristics that are not intrinsic to the genetic code. *Or* perhaps long hair among females, and a beardless face and the 45° "part" among males, *are in fact dictated by the human genome* in the most circuitous of ways, leading our most reputable scientists to cast these *behavioral* characteristics in stone, as it were.

Let us look further at other types of hair grooming behavior that seem to be tied so tightly to the biological gender variable, to see where our analysis leads us.

7. Chest Hair

We have studied human behavior centered around head and facial hair and observed distinctive gender differences. We will now look at grooming behavior directed toward hair on the remainder of the body to see if it conforms with our previous observations.

Although adult males and females both have hair on their chests, it is a predominantly male characteristic. Consequently, we might expect certain similarities in the analysis of *chest hair* with that involved with the facial beard. But we will also discover many differences between the behavioral dynamics surrounding male chest hair and facial hair, and these differences will help flesh out the fundamental differences between males and females.

Generally speaking, chest hair on a woman is not attractive to males or females. Although it is a rare female who has a thick growth of hair on her chest, a substantial number have a few hairs on their chests, often near the nipples of their breasts. In such instances the females will behave to conceal or remove those hairs. This is perhaps all that needs to be noted with regard to female chest hair, except to note that its de-evolution was probably related to the *infant nursing function* which requires unobstructed access to the mother's nipples. Our primary female focus from now on will be with respect to their attitudes and reactions toward male chest hair.

Chest hair is not only a discriminating characteristic between males and females, much like the facial beard, but it also distinguishes men from boys. It appears simultaneously or soon after a male's beard begins to appear. This chest hair is similar to the facial beard in the sense that it varies on a number of dimensions, including its thickness, texture, color, and distinctive distribution across the chest. Like the eyebrows, the natural growth of the chest hair is like a personal signature.

However, unlike the beard, chest hair is generally not shaven off the body except among some body builders who strive to emphasize the conformation of their muscles as a feature to be admired. This chest shaving behavior is more geared toward a limited male peer group than to females, who generally prefer a nominally muscular and hairy chest to an exaggerated muscular build devoid of hair. Since such body building behavior, in its exaggerated form, seems to appeal more to other males than to females, we could hypothesize that homosexuals are disproportionately represented in that subpopulation. In this context it can also be noted that in Hollywood the handful of super-muscular men are seldom "sex symbols" with ardent female followings.

All indications are that a chest of hair is intrinsically appealing to females, just as a woman's breasts are inherently attractive to males. It is not surprising that these gender predilections should have evolved, for ample female breasts are correlated with the ability to bear viable children, and hairy male chests are correlated with the hormone testosterone and the associated traits of strength, endurance, and intimidation of foes—characteristics necessary for the support of the family, in an evolutionary sense.

We will see later that this role of the hairy chest is probably the root evolutionary cause of the *necktie* in the Western world. Few corporate officers want to stand in the board room with their shirt open and exposing a puny chest with hardly a hair, while his subordinates are flashing muscular chests with copious amounts of hair. Again, the covering of the chest results in a *minimization of differences among males,* similar to the cropping of head hair and the shaving of the beard.

But on the *beach* it is a different story altogether, where socio-economic strictures fall apart. The intrinsic appeal of male chest hair becomes apparent when interactions between males and females are observed vis-à-vis their respective characteristics. In general, it will be observed that a hairy chest is correlated with a muscular build, but the overall look is in sharp constrast to the hairless or shaven chest of the dedicated body-builder, which attracts relatively few females. Similarly, there is a sufficient size for female breasts, beyond which they become novelties.

With the exception of the professional body-builders, few males have resorted to grooming behavior directed toward their chest hair, perhaps because its true importance is still not fully documented. No one knows, but in years to come we may well see the grooming of chest hair as extensive as that directed toward the face and head. Once the marketing and advertising worlds see the potential here—never ready to miss a bet—they may introduce chest shavers, chest combs, chest gels, hair growing compounds, depilatories, and all manner of grooming products catering to the needs of those who want to improve upon Mother Nature, in order to get their share of female (or male) attention.

In summary, we see many of the same gender differences with respect to chest hair as we do with regard to the facial beard and moustache. In all cases, such hair growth is undesirable on females, while generally desirable on males.

8. Armpit Hair

Armpit hair is a little studied subject. It is not a common topic of discourse among males or females, suggesting it is not considered of great importance, one way or another. Certainly armpit hair is not treated with the same reverence as the hair on the tops of our heads. Rarely is it braided, or tied in ribbons. Nonetheless, this sadly neglected subject can teach us more about gender dynamics.

We are at a very important world crossroads in the behavioral evolution of armpit hair grooming. The vanguard in this movement is being led by the female population—primarily in America, and to a lesser extent in Europe—just as they were seen to play a leadership role in all types of hair grooming that we have studied so far.

It was the female population, it will be recalled, that initiated behavior patterns aimed at maximizing differences among themselves in an attempt to improve upon their natural traits, whether it was the growing of long hair; curling, straightening, or crimping their hair; coloring their hair; styling it in permuted ways; tweezing and coloring the eyebrows; applying mascara to the eyelashes; or even using a hemostat-like instrument to curl them.

Little of this type of head hair behavior is directed toward armpit hair. In most of the world, females ignore their armpit hair altogether, maybe just giving it an application of deodorant. But the female population in America has chosen to shave their armpit hair entirely. There are exceptions to this armpit shaving behavior, and feminists are among those who have resisted the behavior, though not unanimously; and so the behavior is really too early in its evolutionary development to determine what course it will take.

If the behavior does not die out in a few years, and is passed on to another generation, and if it spreads to other corners of the world, we may be in the process of witnessing an instance of behavioral evolution no less momentous than the beginning of the moustache or the tweezed eyebrow. Until the course of armpit hair grooming becomes more established, it is premature to speculate on something which might only be a passing fancy. Still, it is a behavior which warrants close watching, for such nascent activities often provide insights into their dynamics that are often lost at their later stages of development, when intermediate states no longer exist.

We have observed that worldwide female interest in their armpit hair appears to be in an incipient stage, but *males* have shown little interest in adopting the behavior. Since so few males shave their armpit hair, it is difficult to make observations on whether the hairy armpit or the shaven armpit is the more appealing to females. But as with the other forms of hair grooming that we have observed, it will be the *female population* that determines its course of development through their discriminating reactions toward the practice.

Although our primary concern is with hair grooming behavior, rather than its biological aspects, it is always interesting to speculate on the latter. Certainly everyone knows that the armpits are the site of perspiration glands which can secrete either odorless liquid as a cooling operation, or very stinky fluids during times of anxiety and stress. The underarms as the location of the perspiration cooling mechanism makes sense, in that the lifting of the arms is like the opening of a window. Where else on the body is there this controllable window feature, except perhaps the mouth and anus, which have their own excretion functions.

Why, though, if the armpits are primarily sites of perspiration, do they also have hair. Either the hair is functional or it is a vestige of evolutionary development, serving no purpose whatever. The best way to find out if a variable has an effect is to *change it and watch the consequences.* The leadership role taken by American females in this experiment will be interesting to watch indeed; to see if there are, in fact, dire consequences to the removal of this natural armpit hair, or if it only represents an innocuous removal of a vestigial human feature—perhaps with concomitant benefits related to the attraction of desirable males—and to see whether males in turn will adopt the behavior themselves. Only time can tell.

9. Arm Hair

From a grooming and gender dynamic viewpoint there is not much to be said about *arm hair.* At present there are no significant grooming products or behavior aimed at this hair.

One exception is the female behavior of having their arm hair ''waxed,'' which is an operation in which a waxlike substance is applied to the arms, allowed to solidify, and when it is peeled off, the hair is pulled out by its roots. Supposedly this can be done without the benefit of local or general anesthesia.

Males, on the other hand, show little inclination to remove the hair from their arms. I, for one, have extensive black hair on my forearms extending all the way to the knuckles of my fingers. From personal experience this seems to be a source of fascination for females, both young and old, for many have commented on it with a certain glee in their voice, one young girl giggling about how much I looked like a gorilla. This type of affectionate female behavior suggests to me that thick arm hair on males is something to be desired, not unlike a hairy chest, for its sexual arousal potential.

We are beginning to see a consistent pattern, now, in gender differences related to body hair. Whereas females value the hair on the tops of their heads, they consider other body hair a negative, often acting to remove it. Males, on the other hand, seem to benefit from their body hair, by virtue of the positive female attitudes toward it. We will look at still other body hair sites to see if our preceding observations are supported, before attempting to synthesize them into a meaningful explanatory model.

10. Leg Hair

We have now considered head hair, facial hair, and hair on the upper torso including the chest, underarms, and forearms. Now let us move below our waists and take a look at the hair on our *legs,* before concluding with a consideration of pubic hair.

Generally speaking, males have more extensive leg hair than females. Nonetheless, contemporary females, again led by those in America, have a desire to increase the gap between themselves and the male population by removing all the hair from their legs, thus accentuating the male-female difference.

Female leg hair is the focus of a big business, as can be seen by the considerable range of products designed to remove it. There are straight razors, electric shavers, cream depilatories, electrolysis, the waxing procedure noted above, and most recently a new electrical appliance that pulls the hairs from their roots.

Again, it is important to realize that this leg hair grooming behavior is not universal among women, but is concentrated among the American female population, as with the shaving of the armpit hair. Whether the behavior will spread to other continents on the globe is unknown.

In contrast, few males shave their legs. This seems to conflict with the male habit of shaving the facial hair. We have speculated on various reasons for males shaving off their beards, and it would seem that the same motivations should also apply to the legs, and yet we do not observe much leg shaving among men. The most plausible explanation for this disparity in male behavior toward facial hair and leg hair may rest in the fact that the leg is not visible in the same way as facial hair. But again, male leg shaving may be in a latent stage of behavioral evolution and the future may have surprises in store. In a behavioral evolution sense, we live in exciting times.

So, with respect to the shaving of leg hair we see conclusively that what is not an accepted habit among males is a preferred behavior among females, as we have seen so often before. Although we have not even begun to address gender differences in clothing habits, it is more than relevant to note that females choose clothing styles that will *expose* their legs, and this must somehow be related to their leg shaving behavior. (This type of development of synergistic characteristics is also common in biological evolution.)

The implicit assumption among females is that legs devoid of hair is simply more attractive than hairy legs. Even some feminists who deny gender differences in behavioral capacity are known to shave their legs and regularly wear clothing to expose them. Still, it is too early in the evolution of this female behavior to determine if it will spread to succeeding generations and to other cultures, and become a permanent feature of female behavior.

The most reasonable explanation for the female leg shaving behavior is that males are more attracted to a shaven leg than a hairy leg. This is the kind of question that is best verified with survey research, but anecdotally I can confirm my own preference, as well as that of many other males, for hairless female legs; unless it is fine, blond, angel-like hair, which can be equally attractive, and maybe even more so than a shaven leg. Not coincidentally, *blonds,* genetically, tend to have finer, less extensive leg hair than females with dark hair, and so the female leg shaving behavior may again be aimed at mimicking an accepted standard of beauty, a motive reflected in the high incidence of bleached blonds.

As we are about to conclude our analysis of gender differences in hair grooming behavior, we are forced to wonder whether the differences we have observed are *trivial* and reversible, or are somehow more ingrained and grow out of a fundamental difference in the *genetic* make-up of males and females. And if these dramatic differences exist with respect to hair grooming, *in how many other areas of life do real gender differences exist.* Certainly we can never return to the naïve notion that males and females are essentially alike in their behavioral tendencies and potentials.

11. Pubic Hair

One would think that *pubic hair*, being so close to our crucial reproductive organs, would have considerable significance, and yet I am unable to phantom its function or identify significant gender differences in its grooming.

The single exception is the predominantly female behavior of removing the pubic hair that might be visible when wearing a bikini, and the sometime habit of shaving all the pubic hair. Aside from this, there is little known about pubic hair with respect to gender dynamics.

While the pattern of pubic hair differs from individual to individual, the variation is not so great as that observed for the facial beard, chest hair, or the hair on the head. In an evolutionary perspective, this may be due to the general rule that if a characteristic is *not visible* to potential mating partners—either by itself or as a genetic correlate of a visible feature—it will not influence mating choices and therefore will not evolve along stylized paths to the same degree that visible features do. In this respect, the relatively concealed pubic hair is similar to armpit hair, neither having evolved in stylized paths characteristic of highly visible hair.

The lesson to remember, then, is that if a characteristic is not visible, one way or another, then it stands little chance of having *a differential mating capacity,* with an associated change in the probability that it will appear in the next generation. This in contrast to the potential for evolutionary development and propagation of highly visible genetic characteristics such as the facial beard, head hair, or eyebrows.

Among our unclothed ancestors, the isolated patch of pubic hair may have served the same functions as the modern-day moustache.

12. Summary and Conclusions

We have compared males and females with respect to their behavior toward body hair—including the hair on the *top of the head,* the *face,* the *chest,* the *arms,* the *underarms,* the *legs,* and the *pubic area*—and have uncovered systematic gender differences in *every single instance.*

Most importantly, we noticed that *females* groom their body hair in ways to *maximize the differences among themselves,* and to mimic relatively rare instances of natural beauty, while at the same time distancing themselves from male hair characteristics. These uniquely female behaviors included the growing of relatively *long hair,* its *styling* variation, and its *coloring.* With respect to facial hair, females were found to alter their *eyebrows* and *eyelashes.* In addition, they showed a propensity to *remove all other body hair,* especially the hair of the *underarms* and *legs.*

Male hair grooming, in contrast, was found to be much less extensive, centered only on the *cropping of head hair* and the *shaving of the facial beard,* behaviors which *minimize differences in the male population.*

The fact that females invest much more effort in hair grooming than males, and act to maximize the differences among themselves, suggests that they are *competing for a limited number of desirable males.* This implies that the composition of the female and male populations is quite different, with *more good women than good men.*

In turn, the *limited number of desirable males* vis-à-vis the number of desirable females, is entirely consistent with the theory that *polygamy is the natural order among humans,* as it is with most species in the animal world, representing a *genetic* dynamic that promotes the optimum composition and viability of successive generations.

While at the moment these conclusions may seem preposterous to some, being based solely on an analysis of gender differences in *hair grooming,* we have only begun to document the evidence in its favor.

Chapter 3

Cosmetics Usage

1. Introduction

In the preceding chapter we saw how differently males and females behave with respect to hair grooming. We will now build upon this foundation of gender differences by comparing male and female *cosmetics usage*.

One has only to stroll through the massive cosmetics sections of the local department store, or page through virtually any newspaper or magazine, to get an idea of exactly how many different cosmetics products our society needs for a happy life. In this chapter we will consider the most popular cosmetics and analyze the functions they serve, with a special emphasis on how they fit into the gender dynamics puzzle.

In our study of hair grooming we discovered that females behave in ways to mimic other females who possess universally accepted standards of natural beauty; while the naturally beautiful, in turn, act to further enhance their inborn attractiveness in order to make themselves even more unique. We saw that this behavior tended to *maximize* the variation among females, in contrast to male behavior which tended to *minimize* their differences.

These observations were consistent with the theory that females are in competition for a relatively small number of desirable males—suggesting an *asymmetry* in the male and female populations—which in turn supported the notion that polygamy is the natural order among human beings, just as it is in most of the animal world.

In our following study of cosmetics usage we will look for further gender differences, to see if they add weight to our thesis to this point.

2. Eye Cosmetics

We have already considered a few cosmetic products in our analysis of eyebrow and eyelash grooming. By way of review, we found that males rarely use cosmetics around the eyes, while females do so almost as a second nature.

It was observed that large numbers of females use an *eyebrow pencil* or tweezers to alter the color, density, or natural contour of the eyebrows. This behavior is motivated by the understanding that *eyebrows* are one of the most distinctive features of the face. One need only look closely at icons of beauty—whether female or male—to recognize that these individuals tend to have extremely attractive eyebrows. It is no wonder, then, that females pay so much attention to the grooming of their eyebrows. Why males *do not* is central to our analysis.

Mascara was another hair grooming product that we studied. Its popularity among females was again traced to the motive of imitating the long thick lashes of natural beauties. In addition, we found that females often use a hemostat-like instrument that clamps onto the lashes and curls them. Yet other females apply prosthetic "false" eyelashes. In general, curves are more aesthetically pleasing than straight lines, no doubt accounting for the appeal of long curved lashes, and the variety of means females use to create them.

But there are more eye cosmetics than those related to eyebrow and eyelash enhancement. This should not be surprising, for who can deny that the eyes and the surrounding areas are the most distinctive facial features, and consequently play a large role in a person's personal signature and appeal.

One such product is *eyeliner.* I must admit I don't know exactly how this product is used, but I believe it is in the form of a pencil or brush which is used to paint a borderline on the eyelids at the base of the eyelashes. This, in combination with the mascara, frames the eyes in such a way as to start hearts beating just a little quicker.

The eyes are then further enhanced by applying a substance of various hues onto the eyelids, and though I am not sure what this material is named, I believe it is called *eye shadow.* It comes in various shades of blue, black, red, purple, and just about every other color imaginable. This coloring of the eyelids can then be topped off with some glitter or fluorescent material if additional impact is desired.

The end result of these various eye cosmetic applications is a devastating drop-dead look that will turn the head of any man, and cause other females to shrink in envy. The entire operation takes considerable time and needs to be redone at the start of each day, in addition to intraday touch-ups; but the time and money invested is well worth it, as measured by the rewards it achieves, and its staying power well into the senior years of life.

In contrast, the male population does not yet use much mascara, eyebrow pencil, eyeliner, or eye shadow, but this is not to say that they may not in the future. The dynamics of behavioral evolution, like that of biological evolution, is usually a gradual process, wherein a particular trait spreads through a population slowly and only after its benefits become clearly established. On the other hand, this may be a uniquely female and intractable behavior, *manifesting a primary biological gender difference.* A look at other cosmetics usage patterns might shed further light on this very important evolutionary issue.

3. Rouge

Rouge is a substance that imparts a reddish cast to the cheeks, and again it is associated primarily with female behavior.

It is similar to a product called *blush,* and though I am not certain of the true difference between rouge and blush—and it may only be a semantic difference—they are both used by females to imitate that healthy and attractive red cheek look; the look of rosy cheeks in the winter cold, or a true blush, which is correlated with embarrassment, coyness, flirtation, faint sexual arousal, and other related nonverbal messages. In its most artistic expression it is seen on the faces of the beautiful young girls in paintings by Renoir. Few can deny the appeal of rosy cheeks.

The application of rouge to the cheeks adds a new characteristic to the female face, and it can be made to vary on a variety of dimensions, including its particular shade of red, the expanse of the cheek that it covers, and the contour of its borders. In this respect those females with artistic talent have an advantage over those who just slop it on indiscriminately.

Consequently, rouge offers the opportunity for creating a look even more unique than that afforded by the use of eye cosmetics and hair styling alone. The end result is a *diversification of looks* in the female population, *maximizing the variation among themselves,* and expanding their distance from the typical male look.

After the rouge, mascara, eyebrow pencil, eyeliner, and eye shadow have been applied to the face there are still further opportunities to make oneself more unique, and we will consider them next.

4. Powder

Powder is usually applied to the entire face, again primarily by females, either before or after the application of the rouge; the exact order of the application of which I am not sure, since these are things that women will not reveal even under duress, and therefore must be learned from casual observation alone.

Actually, I believe that there are at least two types of powder, one that is put on before the rouge, as a *foundation* (or maybe that is a cream), and the other after the rouge is applied, to soften the borders and give the whole face that natural look.

The application of powder is, in fact, important in a number of respects. A shiny face is not a healthy face. It suggests that the body is somehow out of balance, as evidenced by the excessive secretion. It may be due to poor diet or stress or a hormonal imbalance, but whatever the case a shiny face is something to be avoided. The application of powder will sop up the excess oils and produce an attractive patina in its place. Powdering of the face among females is so commonplace that there is even a "powder room" allocated to the behavior. If such a room is not available, virtually every female has a *compact case* containing a supply of powder, a powder puff to apply it, and, of course, a mirror to provide feedback on the relative success of the application. If a powder room is not available, it is perfectly acceptable to use the compact case to powder one's face in public.

In addition to eliminating a shiny face and blending in the rouge, the powder can conceal unsightly pimples, or excessively large pores, or even a hint of a moustache.

Powdering of the face, then, is a decidedly female behavior that serves a large number of functions. But it cannot do everything. For some purposes specialized products are needed, as for the lips.

5. Lipstick

Who can honestly deny that full red lips are more attractive than thin colorless ones.

Lips probably differ in as many ways as the eyebrows, and therefore are another personal signature of the face. Males tend to accept the lips with which they were born, but females, as we have seen so often before, have taken the leadership role in behavioral evolution and have found ways to enhance their natural lips.

Lipstick, a fingersized cylinder of pasty substance, available in well over 100 shades of red, pink, and violet, plus every other color, is used by females to enhance the natural state of their lips. It is used not only to color the lips, or to alter their taste and texture, but through artistic license to alter the natural outline of the lips, making them fuller here and thinner there.

Now one begins to understand the full importance of contour in the assessment of beauty, for we have seen efforts to change the curve of the eyebrows, the slant of the eyes, the borders of rouged cheeks, and now the perimeter of the lips, all in an attempt to duplicate the natural, though rarer instances of exceptional God-given beauty. Nothing of value ever goes unimitated. And conversely, we can conclude that what is imitated is of proven value. Lipstick is so important to females, that they will universally admit to the fact that it is the last thing they are likely to leave home without.

We can only imagine the evolutionary origins of painted lips. Most likely it was thousands upon thousands of years ago when a certain young maiden, returning from her berry picking rounds, the juice of a berry or two still on her lips, when she came upon her suitors in the village who were inordinately amorous toward her; and it was not long before her sisters and girlfriends caught onto the ploy, and soon the behavior spread from village to village, country to country, and then to every continent of the globe.

One cannot help but notice that the dynamics of lipstick usage are virtually identical to that of every other cosmetic product that we have studied so far. In every instance the behavior is *uniquely female, widespread, imitative of natural standards of beauty, and maximizes the variation of the female population* vis-à-vis its inborn state. Before we interpret these findings, let us look at other cosmetics usage patterns to make sure our observations have the broadest possible foundation.

6. Perfume

With *perfume* and *cologne*, those scented liquids applied to various parts of the body, we have finally arrived at a cosmetic that is used by both males and females, though the extent of usage, and the variety of products used, is still slanted toward females. Also, there are definite gender differences in the types of scents used by males and females.

Although the gender differences in the usage of perfume is not as dramatic as in the usage of mascara, eyeliner, eye shadow, eyebrow pencil, rouge, and facial powder, the usage dynamics are very much alike.

It is well known that humans can give off foul odors, but it is not so well recognized that humans also exude *tantalizing odors,* especially during moments of bliss or sexual arousal. These subtle and sometimes intoxicating scents are impossible to duplicate in the chemistry laboratory, so parfumers seek materials from other animals, plants, and flowers, as well as synthesized compounds, to create pleasant scents that approach the more subtle human ideal.

Understandably, the created scents vary widely in their appeal. Some differ little from rubbing alcohol, while others cast off exotic smells that appeal to all manner of tastes. Indeed, odors are very similar to food tastes in this respect, and different individuals have completely different preferences. What is a delight for one individual is a gross-out for another.

While some scents may be used to mask a real or imagined body odor, more often it is used to match the best of nature's odors and create an olfactory aura which reaches out and grabs anyone within its range of effect, which can often be large. Indeed, sometimes an individual can leave a trail across an entire room, or, when the wind is right, half a city block.

The key gender differences in the use of perfume have to do both with the *extent* of usage and the *type* of products used. While males will typically splash relatively inexpensive cologne on their freshly shaven faces, or put a dab here and there, females will use perfumes which are more costly and have a distinctly more floral scent. In either case, though, the motivation is not so much to imitate our natural scents, since so few individuals are attuned to these, but the aim is to, on the one hand, give oneself a sense of well-being, and, on the other hand, to enhance one's value in the eyes (noses, actually) of others.

So, even though in this one instance, our observed gender differences are not so great as those already noted, the essential difference still exists and with exactly the same dynamic. That is, females engage in the behavior more extensively than males, and they act in a way to maximize differences among them in their effort to enhance their natural worth to desirable males.

There are many other cosmetics products to consider. Paging through a sample of newspapers and magazines we discover advertisements for such products as *exfoliating scrub, flower petal gel, mud masks, foam wrap, oil of this and oil of that, wrinkle relaxant, line tamer, hydrotherapy, moisture recharging complex, nourishing hydrating emulsion,* plus a line of products touted to "help reprogram your skin to better retain moisture like young skin," with the ultimate marketing conceit found in a product called "simply moisture," all of which suggests a comeback of that age-old favorite, *water.* In yet other advertisements we are told that dermatologists *know* that only 20% of aging—those fine lines and wrinkles—is chronological, and *that 80% is due to environmental effects,* and their products take advantage of "this law of nature" to give you a more youthful skin. The only "law" proven here is that half our magazines and newspapers would fold without the benefit of cosmetics advertising. *Let us pray.*

While there are countless other specialty cosmetic products that we could analyze, not to mention the many forms of cosmetic surgery (which are really too offensive for most sensibilities), our preceding conclusions would only be reinforced. There is, though, one final cosmetic product that is worth discussing, since—unlike certain others—I happen to have a particular weakness for its usage among females.

7. Nail Polish

I doubt that I am alone in my admiration for nicely shaped fingernails coated with almost any color *nail polish*—any shade of red, pink, peach, plum, purple, you name it! Similarly for the toenails.

This particular cosmetic usage, again, is entirely in the female province. It has such appeal among females that the nail polishing behavior often begins in infant girls.

One interesting difference between nail polish usage and the other cosmetic and hair grooming behavior that we have studied, is that the use of nail polish cannot be deemed to be imitative of some natural standard of beauty. Colored nails just do not occur in nature. Here the appeal must be based on certain common aesthetic judgments associated with the appeal of the color and contour of the nails, plus the illusion of longer fingers which are naturally attractive.

By now we no longer need to ask why females practice the behavior and males do not. We have seen too many forms of hair grooming and cosmetics usage behavior that are *uniquely female,* and so well *entrenched* into their lifestyles, that we are forced to conclude that they are *indirect behavioral manifesta-*

tions of a basic genetic difference between males and females.
What is most interesting in this respect is how gender-related
behavior can evolve with essentially the same dynamics as biological and anatomical traits that are unique to either males
or females.

A final cautionary word to males interested in capturing the
good will of a certain attractive female in their lives. Although
her gender-related grooming behavior will now be patently
transparent to you, you must *never, never* let on to her that you
see through her guile, or you are dead in the water. And instead
of concentrating on the impression *your appearance* is making
on her, you now understand that the most important thing you
can do to enhance your stature in her eyes is to tell her sin-
cerely how absolutely great she looks, how much you like the
way she wears her hair, and how much you like her earrings (to
be addressed in the next chapter), and how fantastic her nails
look. This will do infinitely more to reveal your intelligence,
self-confidence, and good taste than any amount of boasting
about your accomplishments, or your hours spent in front of the
mirror trying to beat her at her own game, which in its com-
plexity and internal dynamics is simply impossible to do.

8. Summary and Conclusions

We have compared males with females with respect to their
usage of cosmetics products, including eyebrow pencil, mascara, eyeliner, eye shadow, rouge, powder, lipstick, perfume,
and nail polish.

The most dramatic finding was that there are *clear-cut gender differences* in the usage of these products. In every single
instance, females were found to use these products much more

frequently than males. Indeed, male usage of these products was found to be virtually non-existent.

Secondly, we observed that these cosmetics products are primarily designed and used *to imitate natural and consensual standards of beauty;* for example, mascara for long lashes, and rouge for rosy cheeks. In this context we also noted that a female's artistic ability and aesthetic sense could influence how successful she would be in mimicking any particular standard of beauty—this in addition to her inborn physical attributes.

Thirdly, we found that female cosmetics usage tended *to maximize the differences among females* vis-à-vis what it would be in the absence of such behavior. To understand this dynamic, imagine a classroom of children before and after a Halloween party; or a shelve of books with and without jackets. This diversification of the female population further distances them from the male population, which does not engage in the uniquely female cosmetics usage behavior.

Fourthly, we concluded that the extensive cosmetic-oriented behavior among females, by virtue of its success in maximizing differences among the female population, is motivated by *their competition for the attention of a relatively small group of desirable males.* Although the behavior also serves to enhance one's self-esteem and arouse the envy of other females, the bottomline function is to attract the attention of desirable males.

Fifthly, this unilateral and extensive effort on the part of females to become more unique through cosmetic means, in order to attract a limited number of desirable males, automatically leads to the conclusion that *there are more desirable females than there are desirable males.* This is exactly the same dynamic observed in our preceding analysis of gender differences in hair grooming, where it was found that females act to maximize their differences by growing their hair to widely varying lengths with a variety of styles, and behave in ways to enhance their eyebrows and eyelashes; while males act to minimize their differences by cropping their hair and shaving their beards.

Finally, the strength and consistency of these hair grooming and cosmetics usage gender differences suggest that they are *indirect behavioral manifestations of underlying genetic differences between males and females,* and in conjunction with the above implication of asymmetric male and female populations (wherein there are more desirable females than males), supports the theory that *polygamy is the natural order among humans as it is among other species in the animal world.* A direct corollary is that modern institutionalized monogamy, and its many attendant ills, has failed precisely because of its cultural affront to the biological dictates favoring a polygamous population mating dynamic.

There is always an initial difficulty in capturing a *multidimensional* theory when words must be employed in linear one-dimensional space and time. With so many different ideas flying about, from many different directions, it is helpful to place the concepts under an umbrella label so that the indentification name alone will conjure up the many aspects of the theory without having to explicate them on each occurrence. In this spirit we will refer to the preceding findings and conclusions as the *minimax principle of gender dynamics,* named for the two fundamental gender differences that we have observed—the *maximization* of variation among females, and the *minimization* of variation among males.

The conclusions of the theory, as radical as they may seem to some, would be suspect if they were based solely on the complex of cosmetic behavior observed here, but since the findings of the current behavioral analysis *exactly parallel* those found previously for *hair grooming behavior,* the internal consistency and validity of the theory is buttressed multiplicatively by these presumably independent complexes of behavior.

If we can find a third or fourth area of behavior, independent of hair grooming and cosmetics usage, which submits to the identical analysis, with exactly the same findings, then we are forced to take the theory very seriously, and to examine its implications for our contemporary civilization. Next, we will turn to just such a complex of behavior, *jewelry wearing.*

Chapter 4

Jewelry Wearing

1. Introduction

We have documented clear-cut gender differences in two broad areas of human behavior—hair grooming and cosmetics usage—with essentially identical dynamics. The wearing of *jewelry* offers a third behavioral area that we can analyze to see if it supports the conclusions about males and females found in the preceding chapters, which we have characterized as the *minimax principle of gender dynamics.*

The wearing of jewelry, like hair grooming and cosmetics usage, has evolved independently around the globe, whether in remote islands of the Pacific Ocean, the jungles of the Amazon River basin, the Himalayan highlands, the American plains, the African deserts, the Canary Islands, the Siberian hinterlands, the archipelagic Lesser Antilles, and virtually every place on Earth inhabited by humans.

As such, it is an important area of study in and of itself. But for our purposes, the most important aspect of jewelry wearing—as with hair grooming and cosmetics usage habits—is with respect to differences in behavior between males and females and the dynamics of those differences.

If gender differences are found with respect to jewelry wearing, and if these differences corroborate the observed differences in hair grooming and cosmetics usage, then we come ever closer to being overwhelmed with evidence that these behavioral differences are in fact *biologically based,* manifestations of genetic dispositions, which, in turn, have far-reaching societal implications.

Once we accept the notion that *males and females are basically different,* then our interest is no longer in the presumably superficial behaviors of hair grooming, cosmetics usage, or jewelry wearing, per se, but in the realization that there must be gender differences in *other behavioral areas* as well, and it is these differences that will have implications on how we shape our evolving society.

Indeed, if males and females differ so utterly with respect to the basic behaviors of hair grooming, cosmetics usage, and jewelry wearing, it would be more of a surprise than not, to discover that they do not also differ in other behavioral areas as well. Our intended purpose, then, is not to identify those other behaviors, or their underlying aptitudes, but only to lay the basis for admitting their reality so that others may begin the search, with confidence that they must exist.

Would it not be surprising that the only behavioral ways in which males and females differ is with respect to hair grooming, cosmetics usage, and jewelry wearing? These fundamental behaviors—and not *language, thinking,* or *tool use*—distinguish us from other primates, and yet we surely differ from them in many more important respects. So too must it be with males and females of the human species.

Let us take a look, then, at male and female differences with respect to jewelry wearing to see if it will help to put some of the finishing touches on our accumulating picture of gender dynamics.

2. Necklaces

The *necklace,* whether a simple chain, a string of pearls, or a suspended amulet, is one of the most popular forms of jewelry.

We can speculate again about the evolution of this uniquely human behavior, but the chances are that it evolved independently in different geographic locations on the globe at different times in history. This type of independent evolution of a similar behavior is strong evidence that it is a manifestation of an *inborn genetic potential.*

It may have begun as a garland of flowers, or daisy chain, that one of our enterprising ancestors fashioned, or it may have started as a braided vine, or even a tiger's tail. In fact, any number of scenarios can be imagined for the evolution of the modern necklace in its many variations.

For our purposes, we are primarily interested in why females wear necklaces so much more so than males, and in so many more varieties. Indeed, it has only been in recent history that males have taken to wearing necklaces, and then usually restricted to a simple silver or gold chain, perhaps with a suspended medallion, but rarely a string of pearls or emerald pendant. In contrast, females have been known to wear necklaces for thousands of years, in every variety, as documented by historical and archaeological evidence.

Why males do not wear pearl necklaces, lockets, or chains containing rubies and sapphires, is a question as relevant as why males wear their hair so much shorter than females, and do not use mascara on their eyes. It is yet another confirmation of the *minimax principle of gender dynamics* that we have been observing, wherein female behavior maximizes the variation in their group's appearance; while males act to minimize their variation, or at the very least do not act to create as much variation as females.

Note that the wearing of a necklace alone does not serve to maximize variation among females, for if they all wore, say, a pearl necklace, their variation would not be increased—indeed, it would be decreased—rather it is the fact that they wear all different styles of necklaces that serves to maximize the variation of their population, and simultaneously distances them from the typical male image. Also popular among females are necklaces displaying their "first name," which adds another visible dimension of uniqueness to themselves.

Before we conclude with certainty that jewelry wearing exhibits the same gender dynamics as hair grooming and cosmetics usage, we should study other types of popular jewelry wearing to see if the results are the same as for the necklace.

3. Bracelets

It is a short evolutionary step from fashioning a loop of material for the neck to one for the wrist, creating a *bracelet;* and we will never know for sure which was created first.

From the time of that unknown origin to contemporary society, the bracelet has won virtually universal favor among females and is rapidly growing in popularity among males. Still, the gender differences are pronounced.

Among the relatively small number of males who sport a bracelet, the choice is usually for a simple gold or silver link chain. Females, on the other hand, exhibit a strong behavioral preference for wearing bracelets varying widely in style, ranging from the simple chain, to one embedded with diamonds, rubies, or sapphires.

Also popular among females are large cylindrical bracelets that can be worn around the wrist or used as an armband when worn about the biceps. Few men wear these.

Although it probably rightfully belongs to a category of its own, separate from other bracelets, the wearing of a *wristwatch* is another recent instance of behavioral evolution. Even though it has spread equally to males and females, there are again distinct gender differences in the styles of the watches worn by males and females. The female watches are usually much smaller in size with thinner bands, and the watch department in the local department store should be consulted for a further insight into the nature of the differences. Generally, a female will not wear a characteristically male watch, and a male will not wear a typically female watch.

Another piece of jewelry that is a close relative of the bracelet family is the *anklet*. It is fitted around the ankle instead of the wrist and usually consists of a simple chain rather than taking on the variety of styles characteristic of a wrist bracelet. Wearing of anklets is primarily a female behavior, with few men having yet adopted the practice. But remember that the moustache was laughable when it first appeared, so we cannot categorically rule out the possibility of the evolutionary spread of anklets to the male population.

So, in summary, while males and females both wear bracelet jewelry, the incidence is much higher among females and they exhibit more variation in the styles they wear. In this respect the *minimax principle of gender dynamics* is again supported. Indeed, after studying dozens of individual types of behavior we have yet to find an exception to the rule that females act to maximize the differences among themselves, as well as to maximize their differences from men, while males act to minimize their differences through homogeneous behavior.

If other forms of jewelry wearing conform to this pattern, we will have established it, along with hair grooming and cosmetics usage, as the third major domain of gender differences.

4. Earrings

The behavioral evolution of *earring* wearing is not as easy to phantom as the origins of the necklace and bracelet. The behavior is especially puzzling since it involves the puncturing of the ear in order to attach an ornament.

Still, the behavior must have ancient origins as evidenced by documentary films of remote and isolated tribes who not only puncture their ears to affix ornaments, but also their lips in order to insert a disc the size of a hockey puck. Perhaps the earring spread to modern civilization while the cumbersome lip disc did not, because of how the latter would have put a real crimp in the ability to talk on the telephone or eat at the sushi bar.

Pierced ears, on the other hand, are universally popular among females, even seen among infant girls. However, until very recently, the male population would not even think of wearing earrings. But rock musicians in the Sixties began wearing a single earring and soon the behavior spread to other pockets of the male population, most notably urban homosexuals, and finally to a broader base of the male population, spreading rapidly in regional high school populations, which are veritable crucibles for the development of peer behavior.

Whether the earring wearing behavior among males spreads to a broader base of the adult population, or even to a *second* ear, is still open to question. It could, and then again it might fade away much like the long hair, beards, and far-out clothes of the Sixties gave way to female discrimination, and sanctions in the workplace. Not many earrings are found on males in the corporate boardroom.

Females, in sharp contrast, have firmly established their earring wearing behavior to the extent that virtually every female wears them on a fairly regular basis. And to tell the truth, female earrings are often quite attractive, adding a punctuation to the rest of her facial features. The earrings may range from simple, small, precious stone studs; to ring hoops of enormous size; to complex dangling chandelier-like affairs, my particular favorite.

Again, as with the female hair grooming behavior and cosmetics usage, the wearing of earrings supports the minimax principle of gender dynamics in that it serves to maximize the differences among the female population in their competition to attract the attention of worthwhile males. Indirectly, creation of these unique looks enhances the female's self-image by generating attention from both females and males in general.

Accordingly, the *minimax principle* predicts that the earring wearing behavior among men will not spread, or if it does it will become ritualized into a standardized earring with minimal variation from male to male, and it is unlikely to spread to both ears, without some kind of counter-move among females to maintain their gender distance. In this context it is worth noting that *noserings,* long popular in the East, have begun to be seen among females in Western civilization, with few sightings among males.

There are a variety of other pieces of jewelry such as broaches, hatpins, and barrettes, with similar gender dynamics to those above, but none is so interesting and enlightening as our next topic.

5. Finger Rings

In principle, the *finger ring* is similar to the necklace and bracelet; namely, a loop of attractive material is slipped over an appendage. And although it serves the same functions as discussed above, the behavioral evolution of ring wearing has taken on some novel dimensions of its own, that will crystallize many of the gender dynamics previously observed in our analysis of other jewelry wearing, as well as that of hair grooming and cosmetics usage behavior.

In contemporary civilization different rings have evolved for different purposes. There are those worn in much the same decorative and cosmetic spirit as necklaces and bracelets, but there are also those which signify membership in special groups—*identification* rings. There is the school ring, signifying graduation; the World Series, Super Bowl, and similar rings, signifying achievement in sports; rings associated with religious and fraternal orders; and any number of other "group membership" rings.

The most noticeable difference between male and female ring wearing behavior centers on the *number* of rings worn. Rarely is a man seen wearing more than one ring, while who cannot bear witness to having seen more than a few women wearing rings on every finger of each hand, with some fingers sporting multiple rings. These general purpose rings vary on countless dimensions, and cannot help but attract attention.

But the most interesting rings—since they bear most directly on our subject of gender dynamics—are the *engagement ring* and the *wedding ring.* These rings have quickly run the evolutionary course from the functional, to the stylized, to their current ritualized status, wherein there is little variation in their general appearance, nor in the behavior surrounding their giving and getting, with absolutely no variation in where they are worn, being reserved for the third finger on the left hand. While it is often said that all roads lead to Rome, all human affections, affectations, and related grooming behavior lead to the third finger on the left hand; and so it is a culmination of all that we have learned to this point, and provides additional support for that aspect of the minimax principle of gender dynamics which proposes that female grooming behavior, which always maximizes their differences, represents a competition for desirable males for mating. The engagement and wedding rings are a sign of achieving that goal.

The engagement ring in Western society is given by a male to a female after a courtship and represents the male's commitment to marry her and raise a family. The ring's distinctive feature is a highlighted diamond which can vary in size from the tiny—little larger than the tip of a phonograph stylus—to the impossibly large, approaching the dimensions of a walnut.

Whether the diamond is large or small, the shapes are more or less standard, the basic geometric forms of round, teardrop, or trapezoidal. This standardization of shape, regardless of the diamond's size, introduces an aspect of *perceptual relativity* into the appreciation of the ring; for one can admire the cut independently of the diamond's size in the absence of a comparison ring.

Whereas other types of rings can be worn on either the right hand or left hand, or on any finger one chooses, the engagement ring is worn only on the third finger of the left hand;

which, given the standard and recognizable construction of the ring, represents a redundant ritualization.

The female behavior surrounding the *receiving* of an engagement ring is also fairly ritualized, and often represents the high point of their lives, past and future. The first act is to show it to all her girlfriends, who surround her with excitement and tell her how beautiful it is. All else is anti-climactic, including the wedding invitations, bridal showers, gift registrations, dress selections, cake and flower orders, ceremony site selection, dinner reception arrangements, rehearsals, the wedding, the honeymoon, the pictures, the mortgage, the kids, and then the *divorce*. Sad and cruel, but true.

In the meantime, the engagement ring serves many communication functions. To males, the primary message conveyed by the ring is that the female is no longer open to amorous advances. For the female who was accustomed to much flirtatious male attention, it becomes disillusioning to discover that she will lose that attention; while for the female who never received much male attention, the engagement ring provides her with a rationale for future neglect, and can now display a comforting eat-your-heart-out attitude.

The *size* of the ring also communicates the economic stature of the fiancé, and in other respects acts as a *performance bond,* for if the marriage is not realized it is customary for the female to keep the diamond, for all it's worth, financially and otherwise.

While only females wear engagement rings, both genders wear a wedding ring upon marriage. This ring has also attained the ritualized status of constancy of design, usually a simple unadorned gold band, and it too is only to be worn on the third finger of the left hand.

In addition to serving as a token of their wedding vows, the wedding ring also serves communication functions similar to the engagement ring. The male's wedding band conveys the message to other females that he already has a wife, so they should not expect any serious attention from him. The female's wedding band, worn next to her diamond engagement ring, is an even stronger deterrent to male amorous attention than the engagement ring alone, which at least admitted some possibility for a change in the status quo.

If, as we have concluded, female hair grooming, cosmetics usage, and jewelry wearing, represent a competition for a limited number of desirable males, it is fair to ask why this behavior continues even after that goal is achieved, and why the time and money devoted to grooming is not invested instead in advanced *career training*. The discussion of the dynamics of this apparently ritualized and maladaptive perseverance of exaggerated grooming behavior is left as an exercise.

Despite the significance and joy surrounding the engagement and wedding rings, few of these monogamous marriages succeed, with approximately *fifty percent ending in divorce actions*—usually initiated by the female—with many of the remaining marriages sustained through extramarital diversions of every type, or by religious and socio-economic sanctions. Such a high failure rate in a cultural institution should arouse our suspicions and doubts about the validity and firmness of the foundations supporting that societal convention.

6. Summary and Conclusions

We have considered various forms of jewelry wearing, including necklaces, bracelets, earrings, and finger rings, with the finding that there are *significant differences between males and females* in this area, following the same gender dynamics found for hair grooming and cosmetics usage behavior.

Females of all ages were found to wear all forms of jewelry with much greater frequency than males. Even among those forms of jewelry worn by both men and women, there is much more variation in the jewelry styles worn by females.

These findings further reinforce the *minimax principle of gender dynamics;* the observation that females act to *maximize* differences among themselves, while males *minimize* their differences through homogeneous behavior, as originally observed in hair grooming and cosmetics usage behavior.

These highly consistent gender differences in three broad areas of behavior—hair grooming, cosmetics usage, and jewelry wearing—are believed to be *behavioral manifestations of inborn genetic differences;* in which females are motivated to *compete among themselves for the relatively small number of desirable males.* This disparity in the number of desirable males and females in the population, in turn, supports the theory that *polygamy among humans is the natural order, just as it is in most of the animal kingdom,* for evolutionary reasons which will be discussed later.

Strong support for this theory was uncovered in the observations of the ritualized dynamics surrounding the engagement and wedding rings—the motivational culmination of female hair grooming, cosmetics usage, and jewelry wearing behavior—and which only proved the *untenability of institutionalized monogamy,* as evidenced by the incredibly large number of females terminating their marriages within a relatively short period of time; whereas males propose marriage, females demand divorce.

All of these findings suggest that the age-old practice of polygamy, so successful among other species, but which somehow lost prominence through recent human history—and with disastrous results—be seriously reconsidered as a viable alternative to the failed concept of ritualized monogamy.

Before we turn to a comparison of monogamy and polygamy—including their respective implications for the composition of future generations, as well as their fulfillment of the
human potential—we will study one final area of behavior,
clothing preferences, to see if it substantiates our findings of
gender differences in the areas of hair grooming, cosmetics usage, and jewelry wearing. If this fourth area of behavior also
supports the *minimax principle of gender dynamics,* we will
have accumulated more than enough data in its favor, sufficient
for even the most skeptical, and we can then turn our collective
attention to its most important implications.

Chapter 5

Clothing Choices

1. Introduction

Up to this point we have demonstrated unequivocal gender differences in basic behavior patterns without even considering male and female clothing habits; having concentrated our analysis on the more primitive and universal behaviors of hair grooming, cosmetics usage, and jewelry adornment.

If an analysis of male and female *clothing choices* confirms the findings of our earlier chapters, then we will have forged an airtight case for our theory of gender dynamics; which posits basic genetic differences between males and females and points to polygamy as the natural human order, as it is in most of the animal world.

From the very start it is worthwhile to note that while hair grooming, cosmetics usage, and jewelry adornment are common even among the primitive societies in the hot equatorial regions of the world, clothing there is an alien concept. This supports simplistic and naïve notions that clothes are primarily for keeping warm.

While clothes are certainly necessary to ward off the cold in the seasonal latitudes removed from the equator, we will discover that there is a more multidimensional aspect to them, conforming to the *minimax principle of gender dynamics* already supported by the broad areas of hair grooming, cosmetics usage, and jewelry wearing behavior.

2. Pants

Historically, *pants* have been a uniquely male form of clothing. It is not hard to imagine the evolutionary origins of pants. In the beginning, men no doubt wrapped an animal skin around their shoulders and waist in order to combat the cold. So plausible is this speculation that the stereotype of the ancient caveman always shows him with a skin slung over his shoulder.

But such a skin does not protect the legs and groin area from updrafts of the cold weather. Nor does it protect the legs against thistles and nettles encountered when treking through the forest. Pants, in which the animal skin is *fastened around the legs,* is the ideal solution to the dual threats of cold and thorny underbrush. Add to this the fact that they allow the man to run faster in the pursuit of game or his enemies, and pants were guaranteed a bright future. We see, then, how necessity is indeed the mother of invention.

The evolutionary development of that first pair of pants quickly went through the common stages of *function, style,* and *ritual* to finally arrive in the men's boutique of the local Bloomingdale's and Neiman Marcus department stores, available with pockets, zippers, belt hoops, and cuffs. The *cuffs* no doubt represent a ritualized vestige attributable to the housewife (or cavewife) who was too busy to tailor the pants of her husband to an *exact length;* or it may have been due to the foresight of the mother who realized that the same pants could easily be passed on from father to son, or from son to son, all by virtue of the clever cuff concept—the original *one-size-fits-all* marketing ploy.

Although the wearing of pants among females is a relatively recent phenomenon, there are still major gender differences in the styles worn. While male pants tend to be loose fitting, females generally choose to wear tight-fitting pants which reveal the contours of their *derrieres.* This is consistent with most mammalian behavior in which the female of the species presents her buttocks to males she wishes to attract. Few men can resist this sight, accounting for its popularity.

This gender difference in pants wearing, then, is consistent with the differences observed between males and females with respect to hair grooming, cosmetics usage, and jewelry wearing, and further supports the minimax principle of gender dynamics: loose fitting pants, characteristic of the male population, erase their anatomical differences, making them appear more *homogeneous;* while tight fitting pants among females not only *accentuate their differences,* but distance themselves from the typical male appearance.

3. Dresses

While pants are associated with males, *dresses* are associated with females; so much so that they are the universal labels placed on the doors of public restrooms.

The evolutionary origins of this gender distinction are interesting to contemplate. We have already guessed a plausible functional origin of male pants, and it may shed some light on the evolution of the female dress.

Pants were guessed to keep the male's legs protected from the cold and the forest underbrush, and to facilitate running. Since females were more likely to stay inside the cave or cabin, caring for the children and tending the fire, there was no need for them to go through the extra tailoring effort to change their loosely wrapped animal fur or woven fabric into pant leggings.

As with so much evolutionary behavior, this gender difference in dress wearing moved on from its *functional* stage, through *stylization*, until finally becoming *ritualized*, especially in its erotic leg-baring aspect. Female legs—especially the thighs—are reacted to by males as extensions of the buttocks, accounting for their sexual arousal value.

In this contemporary age, the stylized variety of dresses and skirts, in comparison to the variety of male pants, is so great as to render any further analysis superfluous; except to note that these stylistic variations add just another dimension to female appeal, for what is more attractive than a pretty girl in a pretty dress.

So this modern-day variety of the original female dress—available in literally thousands of styles—is just one more confirmation of the minimax principle of gender dynamics, already substantially documented with observations on hair grooming, cosmetics usage, and jewelry wearing behaviors.

4. Shoes

Some men and women are reported to have hundreds of pairs of *shoes* in their closets. This alone should tip us off to the possibility that shoes serve more functions than the average shoe-wearing mortal can even imagine.

For our present purposes, though, we are primarily interested in any gender differences which might exist in shoe selection and shoe wearing habits, and whether these differences support our earlier findings with respect to gender-related behavior.

Perhaps the most striking difference between males and females is with respect to the wearing of *high-heeled* shoes. Among men, the wearing of high heels is usually restricted to cowboy-style boots, where the high heel functionally serves the purpose of keeping a good grip on the saddle stirrup while riding a horse. In other instances the male high-heeled boot or shoe is a stylized and ritualized offshoot of that original equestrian function, or so it would seem.

The wearing of high-heeled shoes among females is much more common and involves a wider variety of styles. This is entirely consistent with all that we have discovered before—the *maximization of variation* among females, and the *minimization* among males. In comparison with the heels on male shoes, the heels on female shoes vary much more in height, width, and profile.

One motive for females wearing high heels is similar to that found in our analysis of hair grooming and cosmetic usage, the desire to emulate accepted standards of beauty; in this instance the illusion of lengthening of the leg, and achieving greater *stature*—in more than one sense of the word.

Other consequences of wearing high-heeled shoes, in addition to creating the illusion of longer legs, include the flexing and trimming of the calve muscles, the forcing of the derriere to protrude out and causing the breasts to be thrust forward, while creating a small-step gait with an accompanying *clickity-click* sound, achieving an entirely novel profile and rhythm of movement; especially in conjunction with a tight-fitting dress hemmed exactly at mid-thigh, buttocks pumping side to side, while the breasts heave in counterpoint, *ba-boom ba-boom ba-boom*, which in its perfection is a sight to behold.

These many effects of wearing high-heeled shoes among females account for its viability over the years, consistent with the minimax principle which postulates that the maximization of variation among female behavior is designed toward imitating higher standards of beauty and competing with other females for the attention of select males.

Although there are many other interesting styles of shoes that could be analyzed—such as *open-toed* varieties, which are popular among females but rarely seen on males—our conclusions with regard to gender differences would remain the same, so let us step from the tip of our toes to the top of our heads.

5. Hats

Hats often fade from fashion for periods of time but they always come back, and that is no doubt because of the many functions they have served from the beginning of human time.

From an evolutionary perspective the hat no doubt began as a means of keeping the head warm in winter, and, with the addition of a visor or brim, for shading the eyes and face from the sun in summer. From those humble beginnings the hat has gone through all manner of styling changes, with ritualized versions developing among different subpopulations; including the baseball cap, the cowboy hat, the sombrero, the safari hat, as well as various "business" hats.

Females have their own preferences with regard to hat styles, ranging from the tiny pillbox to those broad-brimmed affairs typically associated with Southern belles. In contrast to the male hat styles, the female hats are rarely ritualized to a standard form. Again, the *minimax principle of gender dynamics* reminds us that females would rather die than be caught wearing a piece of apparel remotely resembling that of another female, whether friend or foe. Instead, they will choose from among hats that vary in the size and shape of its crown and brim, as well as in terms of decorative flourishes including feathers, hatpins, or veils; features rarely seen on the standard male headgear. In any case, a hat choice, like a hairstyle, makes a statement about a person's personality or mood, not otherwise readily apparent.

One possible reason why hats are not as popular among females as, say, high heeled shoes, might be that hats compete with their hair styling, in which they have invested so much time and effort. This may also explain why hat wearing is more common among more mature women, who do not exercise as many hair styling variations as younger females, and place relatively less importance and pride in their hair which they feel has lost much of its youthful luster.

Another important function of hat wearing is to make the wearer appear taller. A hat, in conjunction with high-heeled shoes, can turn a person of low stature into a veritable pillar of admiration, whether male or female.

Incidentally, one little realized benefit of the hat is its ability to reduce anxiety. By its snug fit on the *brow* and the *temples,* the hat provides *feedback* at those times when we are stressed and wrinkle our brow or experience an increase in heartbeat. Normally we are unaware of flexing our forehead muscles during anxious states, or of an increase in our pulse, but with a tightly fitting hat, we immediately get feedback informing us of our tense state of mind, and can act to relieve it, more so if we are attuned to it.

The headband, which has grown in popularity in recent years, also serves this same self-regulating homeostatic feedback function, in addition to its stylistic function of attracting attention; since our eyes are naturally drawn to borders.

So, while hats are not universally worn by either males or females, we still observe distinct gender differences in their usage. This adds to our accumulation of evidence that gender dynamics with respect to clothing are the same as that for hair grooming, cosmetics usage, and jewelry wearing.

6. Shirts and Blouses

We will consider the *shirt* and *blouse* together, since they are essentially the same piece of clothing and the major differences that do exist are related to our prime interest of gender differences.

In terms of similarity, they are both garments to cover the upper body from waist to neck, with buttons on the front, and, in the case of long sleeved versions, buttons on the cuffs. (As an exercise in the dynamics of behavioral evolution, contemplate why zippers are used on pants and skirts, while buttons are used on shirts and blouses.) Despite their broad similarities, the shirt and blouse, even in name, are, respectively, male and female garments.

The male shirt is of a fairly standard design, including the size and spacing of the buttons, the generally loose fit, and a ritualized turned-down collar of standard design. The sleeves extend either to the wrist (long-sleeved shirts) or only to the bicep (short-sleeved shirts). The buttons are approximately a half inch in diameter, and spaced 3½ inches center to center, and are placed on the right hand side of the garment. There are also buttons on the sleeve ends, which fasten together a seven-inch longitudinal slit in the sleeve. The evolutionary origins of this feature have not been documented, but it is believed that the function of the buttoned cuff is to allow the rolling up of the sleeves, which we men are wont to do when we get down to the business at hand.

The blouse is the female counterpart to the male shirt. As predicted by the minimax principle of gender dynamics, the female blouse varies considerably in comparison to the male shirt. While the male shirt is most likely to be made of cotton or polyester fabric, blouses are also common in a variety of other materials including silk, rayon, and nylon. The length of the blouse sleeve also varies considerably more than the male shirt, ranging from a wrist-length version, all the way to a sleeveless version, with a continuous range in between. The fit on the body varies considerably from very snug to very loose. Also, they are often embellished with pleats, lace, uniquely shaped collars, and any variety of buttons.

These observed differences between the male shirt and female blouse are entirely consistent with the gender differences found in our analysis of shoes, hats, pants, and dresses, and lends further support to the minimax principle of gender dynamics; already on solid ground, based on an analysis of male and female differences in hair grooming, cosmetics usage, and jewelry wearing.

7. Neckties

In terms of behavioral evolution and gender dynamics, the *necktie* is one of the most interesting and enlightening of phenomenon.

Unlike other garments which have male and female counterparts—as if clothing differences evolved in parallel with differences in sexual organs—the necktie is a peculiarly male garment. Although its evolutionary origins are not proven, it is tempting to speculate on how it reached its current universal status.

An admittedly apocryphal account of the origins of the necktie has it that a certain Lars Johanson of Minneapolis, Minnesota, arrived at his place of employment one morning in the dead of winter, and after taking off his coat and hat, left his scarf wrapped around his neck to ward off the marked chill of the office, due to an accidental breakdown of the furnace. Throughout the morning, the females in the office all complimented him on the attractiveness of his scarf. The next day he arrived at the office wearing another stylish scarf that his mother had knit for him, and though the office was nowhere as chilly as the preceding day, he wore the scarf all day long, again attracting the attention and compliments of the female employees, while the other men in the office stood in the corner grumbling and muttering among themselves.

The next day, these other male employees arrived at work wearing their best scarves and continued to wear them throughout the day, commenting on how chilly it was in the office, even though the furnace had now been repaired. In so doing they captured their share of female attention, to which they were rightfully entitled. The scarf-wearing behavior continued day after day and spread from one department to the other— how easy it was to attract the attention of the girls in the office. As summer approached the men adapted by asking their mothers to fashion scarves that were not quite as heavy as the winter versions, and soon the neck scarves became lighter, thinner, and less bulky.

Although there are no records of continuous intermediate forms, the necktie is presumed to have evolved from these *functional* beginnings, through *stylized* changes, and finally arriving at its contemporary *ritualized* form; guaranteeing it a spot in the behavioral evolution hall of fame.

Quite independently, the importance of the necktie can also be related to our discussion of hair grooming behavior. It will be recalled that male chest hair was seen as a correlate of male attractiveness, but according to the *minimax principle of gender dynamics* the differences among males will tend to be minimized by their behavior, with the result that, for instance, barechested subordinate males could not upstage the senior vice presidents or department heads in the staff meeting room.

So, the necktie successfully serves the purpose of concealing male differences in chest hair, and through the *ritualized constancy of the necktie design* further homogenizes the male population vis-à-vis the female population; which, as we have seen over and over again, behaves to *maximize* their differences. If females do occasionally wear a tie, it is a stylized version of the male standard, more like a scarf than anything else, with many more degrees of variation.

In this context it is interesting to observe how the *shirt collar* and *necktie* play synergistic roles; the necktie holding the shirt tight at the neck, and the folded-down collar holding the tie in place. In addition to the function-style-ritual course that much behavioral evolution follows, this type of *inter-characteristic dependency* is also observed as behavioral constellations become more complex. We also saw it with respect to the leg-shaving and short-dress behavior of females, as well as in the development of the portable cosmetics compact kit. The evolution of the female *purse*, from its functional beginnings for carrying essential items such as the compact and lipstick tube, through its stylized changes, to its current ritualized status, is yet another instance of this inter-dependency between behavior patterns.

So, while the necktie at first glance appears to be the first observed violation of the minimax principle of gender dynamics, in that unique neckties seem to serve to *differentiate* among males, upon closer inspection is found to be entirely consistent with the male homogenization dynamic, by virtue of the ritualized rigidity of the necktie design; which in addition to creating a *constancy of fashion,* serves *to conceal discriminating features of the male chest.*

Females, in contrast, are prone to wear their blouses open to reveal varying amounts of flesh, or actual cleavage of their breasts; fully consistent with the minimax principle which posits that females maximize the differences among themselves in competition for the attention of a few select males, and for this we are forever grateful.

The large number of instances of these types of gender differences, observed in the disparate behavioral complexes of *hair grooming, cosmetics usage,* and *jewelry wearing,* in addition to *clothing choices,* strongly suggest that the observed behavioral differences—so dramatic and consistent in their nature—are not arbitrary cultural differences but represent *manifestations of genetic gender differences.*

The nature of the differences, wherein females act to maximize their differences, *without comparable behavior among males,* leads to the conclusion that the female behavior is motivated by *a competition for a limited number of desirable males.* The implied disparity in the compositions of the male and female populations, and the nature and strength of the gender differences, support the theory that *polygamy is the natural order among humans* as it is in most of the animal world.

We will address these conclusions at greater length in the concluding chapters. In the meantime, to round out our discussion, we will consider a few additional differences in gender clothing behavior which will further support the minimax principle and its implications.

8. Suit Jackets

We can abbreviate our discussion of the gender dynamics surrounding the *suit jacket* because it almost exactly parallels the analysis of the necktie in its details.

Like the necktie, the suit jacket with matching pants is primarily a male garment. Among the smaller number of females who wear such suit jackets, they may wear either matching pants or a skirt, but often with unique styling flourishes.

In contrast, virtually all male suits are *identical* in design, serving to homogenize men in accordance with the minimax principle. Among the most interesting aspects of the suit jacket is how the folded down collar, or *lapel,* has evolved to its current ritualized form with a constancy that changes only slightly from one decade to the next, at one time being relatively thin and at other times widening. Despite the slight variation in width over time, the lapel maintains its same characteristic angular outline.

In contrast, female suits, while bearing some semblance to the male suit, vary considerably in tailoring, lapel design, and color. Because of its relatively standard design, almost like a uniform, the suit jacket is not widely popular among females, since it violates the dictates of the minimax principle that the female tendency is to make themselves more unique, whether it is through hair grooming, cosmetics usage, jewelry wearing, or clothing choices.

As alluded to above, the male suit is of such standardized design that it is virtually a uniform. It has become so ritualized that it is even worn in the middle of summer with temperatures approaching 100 degrees Fahrenheit.

With the institutionalization of the uniform male *suit,* in conjunction with the typical male *shirt* and *necktie,* along with closely *cropped hair,* the *"part,"* and a *shaven face,* the male population has evolved to a state of similarity that seems to be terminal in nature, with little opportunity for further homogenization except the *shaven head,* which we predict is next. In marked contrast, the female population has achieved a maximum of heterogeneity through variation in *hair grooming, cosmetics usage, jewelry wearing,* and *clothing choices.*

While we are on the subject of jackets, it is of interest to note in passing that with respect to outer coats, the *fur coat* is especially interesting in that it has evolved full circle from its early functional cave-dweller origins, to its current stylized version, representing the apogee of contemporary female fashion.

It is worthwhile to take one final look at the male suit-and-tie look, to gain insight into the dynamics of the behavioral evolutionary process. Over and above its ritualized constancy, it is interesting to analyze the *particular form* that it has taken in Western society, as compared to alternative uniform dress codes in other cultures. Here we see certain *principles of aesthetics* dictating the course of development of the standardized Western look. The *triangle,* for instance, is widely regarded as an aesthetically pleasing form. As an exercise, take a look at the typical suited male, and count the number of triangles that appear in the lapel, shirt collar, necktie, and the areas between them. See for example, Figure 5.1. Discuss your results in the context of *chance* vs. *systematic* evolutionary development, and *learned* vs. *inborn* perceptual preferences.

Although there are a multitude of other garments and accessories that we could analyze with respect to the minimax

Figure 5.1—Clothing of Modern Man.

principle of gender dynamics, we will conclude our study of clothing with just a few more of the most interesting areas.

9. Underwear

A visit to the lingerie department of the local department store will show just how differently males and females are with respect to their *underwear* choices.

The stylistic variations in female stockings, panties, garter-belts, girdles, bras, and teddies are enough to fill entire catalogs. No true male can deny the attractiveness of these garments, and when they are worn by an attractive female the effect can be devastating on the man. I get warm just thinking about them; proof of their potency.

Since these undergarments are worn by females of all ages, and in most instances are never even seen by another person, one could argue that this is one refutation of the minimax principle of gender dynamics, which proposes that females maximize their differences in order to compete among themselves for the attentions of select males. How could this be a motive if, in many instances, the underwear is never even seen by males. On the surface this is a valid argument, but we should always be wary when an exception is used to discount a rule, which is otherwise supported by overwhelming evidence. Indeed, except in physics, the exception proves the rule.

Even in this instance we can find support for the proposition that the motive behind the wearing of stylized undergarments is to attract males, even if they can't see them. To fully understand this, one really has to be intimately familiar with the strange forms that female logic can take, as well as the dynamics of the shopping experience.

But since a gender difference in the capacity for logical thought is not our prime topic of study, and since it cannot be quickly documented here like differences in hair grooming, cosmetic usage, jewelry wearing, and outerwear choice behavior, we cannot presently resort to it as support for the seemingly unlikely proposition that stylized female underwear is worn to attract males, considering that men often cannot even see the undergarments. To understand how this can indeed be the bottomline motive, recall that we have often observed that uniquely female behavior also serves the autoerotic function of enhancing their self-esteem, and once it is accepted that such a boost in self-esteem *translates into observable behavior,* whether in terms of one's *gait, posture, eye movements, speech,* etc., then the male-attracting motive is no longer as illogical as it may have seemed at first glance.

Certainly if males can imagine a female's undergarments, a female can imagine *a male imagining* that he can actually see them. Besides, females often wear outer garments and posture themselves so snatches of their underwear can be seen by ever-attentive male eyes. Certainly panty outlines in their many varieties are clearly visible through outer garments. And who can deny that a nicely shaped bra, whether stuffed with tissue paper or with nature's own endowment, when worn beneath a snug sweater or dress, is essentially visible in many respects, and when worn with the typical translucent blouse is clearly visible.

Here we can speculate that the *bra* evolved not just to brace the bust, but to create the illusion of naturally firm, conically shaped, cantilevered breasts; and this is entirely consistent with other female grooming behavior which we have seen to mimic natural standards of beauty. Yet another aspect in the evolutionary development of the bra, could be its function of concealing *erect nipples* which often tip off a female's sexual arousal. Note, too, that the braless and see-through blouse fashion of the Sixties did not last very long at all.

So, while the wearing of stylized underwear, apparently invisible to observers, seems to challenge the aspect of the minimax principle which posits that the maximization of variation among females is aimed at attracting select males, the implication still holds and must be entertained until a better theory of invisible stylized female underwear is advanced, and which also explains unilateral gender differences in hair grooming, cosmetics usage, jewelry wearing, and outer clothing behavior.

10. Color Preferences

We have identified dramatic gender differences in every variety of clothing behavior, including that related to shoes, hats, pants, skirts, dresses, neckties, suits, and underwear, and these differences were found even without recourse to differences in color preference behavior. If we can also find similar differences between males and females with respect to their clothing *color choices,* we will have added yet another dimension to the accumulating support for the minimax principle of gender dynamics.

How or why color vision evolved is both a biological and behavioral question, but beyond the scope of our presentation. Our interest is primarily in the *existence* of gender differences in color preferences and the implications of those differences.

The differences between males and females in color usage is so pronounced that it is difficult to know where to start. Certainly the differences are clearly noticeable in the contemporary workplace. Who has not seen senior female executives enter the staff or board meeting room on many occasions wearing bright *yellows, reds, pinks,* and *purples.* And yet, despite their greater numbers, few male executives will be found with *lavender* or *fuchsia* suits. Why is this?

We have already observed that the male population is homogenized by its uniform suit tailoring, standard-shaped necktie, cropped hair with a "part," and shaven face. The minimization of variation among males is further accomplished by a narrowing of clothing color choices. Only the necktie is allowed a pastel color, and then usually restricted to red and yellow. The shirt is usually white, or, if colored, the faintest possible shade. The matching suit jacket and pants—the main components of the male uniform dress code—is restricted to *blue, gray,* and *brown.* While they often contain stripes of another color, rarely does a male suit have floral or paisley patterns, common among female wardrobes.

Among females, the choice of clothing colors is dramatic. Although they wear the same blue, gray, and brown male color choices, they more often choose bright floral pastels including various shades of green, orange, yellow, red, pink, purple, violet, ochre, mauve, and magenta. Everyone will agree that these bright colors attract more attention than blue, gray, and brown, and one begins to realize that comparisons between attractive girls and flowers have more than a little basis in reality.

In grade school we learned the colors of the spectrum, but we never learned their associated *psychological* and *communicative* significance. Given that there are such strong gender differences in color preferences, it is worthwhile to get an idea of the meanings of various colors. Here we closely follow the conclusions of pioneer Swiss color researcher Max Lüscher.*

*Lüscher, Max. *The Lüscher Color Test,* English translation, Random House, New York, 1969.

While *red* signifies action, desire, and competitiveness; *blue* is passive, balanced, and content. And whereas *yellow* is expansive, hopeful, outgoing, and cheerful; *green* tends to be proud, stubborn, persevering, and self-centered. Among the secondary colors, *pink* is total confidence, when all is right with the world. In contrast, *purples* and *violets,* are more oriented toward fantasy, wish-fulfillment, and the fanciful, and are disproportionately preferred by children and homosexuals of both genders. Among the drabber colors, *brown* is a failed or frustrated red, representing caution, compensation, and insecurity; while *gray* is neutral in tone, suggesting a guarded, undecided, or noncommittal attitude. Among the achromatic colors, *white* represents purity, innocence, and new beginnings. *Black* is the most difficult to characterize, since it can represent the absence of color altogether, or the sum total of all colors. Depending on its context, black can variously suggest negativity and withdrawal, a terminal funereal state, a religious ascetic identification, or even a transcendent innocence, much like white; so its context is even more important for its interpretation than for the other colors.

In the context of gender differences—in addition to differences already observed—it is worthwhile to note that infant girls are usually associated with *pink,* while boys are associated with *blue;* with *yellow* representing a more neutral gender color.

Irrespective of the psychological meanings and communication values of colors, the great gender differences in clothing color choices further support the *minimax principle of gender dynamics,* which notes that females act to maximize the differences among themselves, while males act to minimize their differences. This one-sided effort on the part of the females to be more unique implies that they are in competition among themselves to attract the attentions of a limited number of valued males; and this disparity in the number of desirable males and females in the population supports the notion that polygamy is the natural order among humans as it is in most of the animal world. Furthermore, this conclusion is reached even without recourse to the fact that the opposing institution of monogamy has proven to be a total failure, both for individuals and society as a whole.

Before we discuss the implications of these conclusions more thoroughly, we must consider one final clothing behavior which will crystallize all that we have covered so far.

11. Formal Wear

It is appropriate that we conclude our discussion of gender differences in clothing behavior with a consideration of *formal wear,* for it represents the high watermark of fashion, and provides the *coup de grace* in our defense of the minimax principle of gender dynamics.

All of the gender differences we have discussed to this point come to the fore during formal gatherings of males and females. Very quickly we notice that the males all look alike, more so than even during a typical business day, for during these "black-tie" occasions the men do not even have the opportunity to choose a uniquely colored necktie, and their characteristic blue, gray, or brown suit is now even more ritualized into the *uniformly tailored black tuxedo;* all this in conjunction with their closely cropped hair and shaven beard. This, of course, will be recognized as the ultimate in male homogenization dictated by the minimax principle of gender dynamics.

In sharp contrast, the variation among the females at these formal gatherings is at its maximized outer limit. Each wears a distinctive hairstyle, a day in the making; each has applied every available cosmetic, plus secret ones imported by their private cosmeticians from the remote highlands of Tibet; each is wearing precious jewelry around the neck, wrists and fingers, valued in excess of the tax base of the typical community in the state of Iowa; and each is wearing a unique one-of-a-kind dress, designed particularly for this occasion; and who really knows what kind of undergarments they are wearing.

Here, then, we see the behavioral evolution of the ritualized monogamous society in all its aspects. We see in clear relief the minimax principle of gender dynamics in its exaggerated form, wherein females act to maximize differences among themselves, while males act to minimize their differences, to the limiting degree. To the extent that the females already have a male mate, their unique grooming behavior has gone beyond the functional role of attracting a valued man, and has taken on a life of its own, as most habitual forms of behavior do, even when the antecedents no longer exist.

Ironically, in this formal setting of ritualized monogamy, the one feature of these women that is *not unique* in appearance is their homogenized male companion; and in turn, the only external mark of distinction among the males is their finely groomed female mate. It is as if the females conspired among themselves to dress their male mates in a bland mode, so as not to divert any attention away from themselves. This, then, is an appropriate conclusion to our overwhelming evidence in support of the *minimax principle of gender dynamics.*

12. Summary and Conclusions

In this chapter we have studied gender differences in clothing choices, and found that the distinctions between males and females in clothing behavior parallel those found in earlier chapters with regard to hair grooming, cosmetics usage, and jewelry wearing.

Differences between males and females with respect to particular types of behavior would be interesting in itself, but when those differences are *dramatic* and follow a *consistent pattern*, then we are forced to stand up and take attention. We have found that the differences can be summarized by the *minimax principle of gender dynamics*, which observes that females act to *maximize* the differences among themselves, while males behave to *minimize* their differences.

This gender dynamic implies that females are *competing* with one another for a *limited number of choice males*, and in its strength and consistency represents a *behavioral manifestation of an inborn genetic tendency*. This in conjunction with the implied disparity in the number of desirable males and females in the population, strongly suggests that *polygamy is the natural biological order among humans* as it is in most of the animal world. This conclusion is independently buttressed by the genetic mathematics of polygamy, and the wholesale failure of ritualized monogamy with its attendant societal ills.

In the concluding chapters we will look at these conclusions in more detail and present their implications for both the cultural and biological evolution of the world population.

Chapter 6

The Minimax Principle
Of Gender Dynamics

1. Introduction

We have compared males and females of the human species with respect to four broad categories of behavior; including hair grooming, cosmetics usage, jewelry wearing, and clothing preferences.

Huge gender differences were found in each instance, and these differences were shown to follow a consistent pattern, which we characterized as the *minimax principle of gender dynamics;* wherein females are found to behave in ways which will *maximize* both the variation in the differences among themselves and their differences from the male population, while males act to *minimize* the variation among themselves.

These dramatic well-documented gender differences in presumably independent areas of behavior—hair grooming, cosmetics usage, jewelry wearing, and clothing preferences—and their imperviousness to change, represent overwhelming support for the proposition that these behavioral differences are manifestations of *underlying genetic differences* between males and females.

The nature of the gender differences—females acting to make themselves more unique, and males acting to homogenize themselves—is consistent with the interpretation that the female behavior represents *competition among themselves for a limited number of desirable males.*

This female competition for a relatively small number of select males, along with the genetic underpinnings of the behavior, strongly suggests that *polygamy is the natural order among humans* as it is in most of the animal world. This interpretation is further supported, and independently so, by the broad-based *failure of monogamy,* with its attendant societal malaise; most notable among the female population.

In this chapter, we will review and expand on the data in support of the minimax principle of gender dynamics, and further discuss its many aspects and some of its more important logical consequences. Then, in the final chapter, we will consider its most important implication, an analysis of alternative population mating dynamics and their evolutionary consequences; with special emphasis on contemporary societal ills attributable to modern civilization's failed experiment with ritualized, rigidified, and institutionalized monogamy.

Although these final chapters could well stand alone, without benefit of the preceding chapters, the salience of these logical conclusions would suffer in the absence of those detailed inductive developments.

2. Behavioral Gender Differences

We set out to find *clear-cut differences* between male and female behavior, rather than grapple with marginal and perhaps illusory differences. This is because dramatic differences between groups help us to uncover the basic distinguishing characteristics of those groups, while studies of marginal differences present the dual difficulty of unequivocally verifying those differences and attributing much significance to them. On the other hand, large differences between groups—males and females, in this case—are more likely to give us insight into all aspects of their behavior; for in most areas of study, when we thoroughly understand the basics, we intuitively know the rest.

Hair grooming. We began our study of behavioral gender differences by comparing males and females with respect to hair grooming habits. We found marked differences ranging from the comic to the profound.

With respect to the hair on our heads, we observed clear gender differences in both hair *length* and *styling*. Females, as a group, were found to grow their hair much longer than males, and also styled it in a wider variety of ways. These were not marginal differences requiring statistical hypothesis testing, but clear-cut differences that could be universally documented by inspection alone.

Among the most interesting of our observations was the characteristic way in which males *part their hair on the side of the head*, demonstrating the way in which human behavior can evolve through the same function-style-ritual sequence observed in various other species of animals.

In terms of facial hair, additional gender differences were uncovered. Most notable was the exclusively female behavior of grooming the *eyebrows* and *eyelashes*. With respect to exclusive male behavior, the shaving of the *beard* was found to be a significant type of behavior since it tended to make males more homogeneous as a group.

Behavior toward body hair was yet another source of gender differences. Females, much more so than males, were found to shave their *armpits, legs,* and *pubic hair.*

These large and consistent gender differences in behavior directed toward the hair on the head, face, and body, was considered to be significant in itself, and would be even more significant if male and female differences could also be found in other forms of behavior as well—which they were.

Cosmetics usage. In addition to the female usage of cosmetics on the eyebrows and eyelashes, noted above, they were also found to use *eyeliner* and *eye shadow* products for the area surrounding the eyes. In addition, usage of *rouge, perfume,* and *nail polish* was found to be a very frequent form of behavior among females.

In sharp contrast, males were rarely observed using any of these products. These dramatic gender differences, in conjunction with those found with respect to hair grooming behavior, began to reveal a consistent pattern in gender differences, too systematic to be attributed to chance.

Jewelry wearing. Next, even further behavioral differences were found between males and females with respect to the amount and types of jewelry that were worn.

We considered the wearing of *necklaces, bracelets, armbands, earrings, noserings, anklets, broaches, barrettes,* and most significantly, *finger rings.* Without exception, females wore each type of jewelry more frequently than males and in a wider variety of styles. Indeed, in many instances such as pearl necklaces, broaches, anklets, and barrettes, hardly any males were found to wear these types of jewelry.

These glaring gender differences in jewelry wearing, in conjunction with those found with respect to hair grooming and cosmetics usage, were so similar in their dynamics that the case for a genetic causation of these differences became more and more plausible.

Clothing choices. Differences in the types of clothing worn by males and females was the fourth broad area of behavior that was studied, to see if such differences existed and whether they were consistent with those found for hair grooming, cosmetics usage, and jewelry wearing behavior.

We found unusually large gender differences with respect to a wide variety of clothing behavior, including the wearing of *shoes, hats, pants, skirts, dresses, shirts, blouses, neckties, suit jackets, underwear,* and *formal wear.* Not only did we discover major differences between males and females in terms of the *types* of clothing worn, but there were corresponding differences in the variety of *colors* worn.

The sheer number of behavioral gender differences in clothing habits—when added to the many specific differences in hair grooming, cosmetics usage, and jewelry wearing—forced us to postulate that these differences were indeed manifestations of *underlying genetic differences* between males and females. We know we are observing a reliable phenomenon when it repeats itself over and over again; replicability being the hallmark of reliable observations. The probability of observing so many gender differences, if in fact males and females were behaviorally the same, is so remote as to defy consideration.

The minimax scale. Of the large number of gender differences that we studied, some are more potent discriminators than others. We can summarize the major distinguishing gender variables with the following list of ten highly visible behavioral characteristics:

- *Long hair on the head*
- *Lipstick*
- *Eye cosmetics*
- *Cheek rouge*
- *Earrings on both ears*
- *Necklace* or *broach*
- *No necktie*
- *No suit jacket* (or, *a red, green, yellow, pink, or purple one)*
- *Exposed leg flesh* or *carrying a purse*
- *High-heeled shoes*

These ten behavioral characteristics can be used to form a scale—*the minimax scale*—which will reliably discriminate between males and females. For any individual it is only necessary to count a 1 for the presence of each of the above ten binary characteristics, resulting in a total score ranging anywhere from 0 to 10.

Individuals who score *above 5* on the minimax scale are most probably *female,* while those scoring *5 or lower* are most probably *male;* with relatively few errors of classification. The use of this type of scale to differentiate group membership, and to understand their basic differences, is referred to as a *discriminant function,* and is discussed in far greater detail in my textbook *Statistical Analysis: An Interdisciplinary Introduction to Univariate and Multivariate Methods.* It is left as an exercise to word the above ten discriminating variables more precisely—for example, what exactly defines ''long'' hair, or ''high'' heels.

Although we did not study other possible behavioral gender differences, it would seem very unlikely that such differences do not exist, given the dramatic differences that we have un-covered in the above four behavioral areas; namely, hair groom-ing, cosmetics usage, jewelry wearing, and clothing choices. Indeed, it would be highly remarkable if these observed be-havioral differences represented the sum total of all gender distinctions.

Most importantly, we have discovered that the observed gender differences are not just distinctions in kind or quantity, but actually follow a well-defined pattern, which we labeled the *minimax* principle of gender dynamics, for its key features, which we will consider next.

3. Maximization of Female Variation

The minimax principle of gender dynamics is based in part on the observation that female conduct in a number of indepen-dent categories of behavior—hair grooming, cosmetics usage, jewelry wearing, and clothing choices (each composed of a large number of more specific forms of behavior)—follows a consistent and predictable pattern, wherein the end result of their actions is to *maximize* the differences among themselves in appearance, as well as their differences from males.

This maximization of variation among the female popula-tion was achieved in a wide number of ways. With respect to the hair on the head, we found that females grow it to every possible length, with an average length well in excess of the average male's. To further accentuate their hair, females were found to practice all manner of styling variations includ-ing curling, straightening, waving, braiding, crimping, bleach-ing, and coloring, behaviors relatively unknown among the male population.

Females further differentiated among themselves by plucking and penciling their eyebrows to create a new look; adding mascara to their eyelashes to make them longer and thicker than their natural lashes; and using eyeliner and eye shadow products to vary the appearance of the areas surrounding the eyes.

One form of female hair grooming behavior which does not totally support the minimax principle is the shaving of the armpits and legs, which, if anything, serves to reduce variation in appearance, much like the male face shaving habit. But, since in human behavior, the exception proves the rule, we should not dwell unduly on this single departure from the minimax principle. In this context it should be noted that the armpit and leg shaving behaviors do support the minimax corollary that female grooming behavior is designed to imitate and exceed accepted standards of beauty. So, just as naturally blond head hair is so often imitated among females, the seemingly "hairless" legs of blonds is also emulated. Furthermore, this female leg shaving behavior is not totally an exception to the minimax principle, since it does serve to differentiate females from the hairy-legged male population; maximization of female differences from males being a central component of the minimax principle.

So, with a minor exception, we see how female *hair grooming* behavior achieves a maximization in the variation among their population. Add to this the increased variation contributed by *cosmetics usage*, involving hundreds of shades of rouge, lipstick, and nail polish, we see conclusive support for the minimax principle.

The wide variety of female appearances achieved by hair grooming and cosmetics usage behavior is multiplied by the wearing of many different types of *jewelry*, fashioned from such precious materials as gold, silver, diamonds, rubies, emeralds, and sapphires, to mention a few; as well as less precious materials such as carnelian, jade, amethyst, lapis, onyx, and cubic zirconia. The jewelry takes the form of necklaces, bracelets, anklets, barrettes, broaches, earrings, nose rings, and finger rings.

As if hair grooming behavior, cosmetics usage, and jewelry wearing were not sufficient to achieve maximum variation among females, they were also found to wear *clothing* that differed widely in both *style* and *color*.

To fully understand this component of the minimax principle—namely, the maximization of variation among females—we can conduct a little *thought experiment*. To determine the effect of a variable, we need only to change it systematically and observe the consequences. Imagine for a moment a random sample of a hundred females standing in a row. Notice their clothing styles and colors, their jewelry, their cosmetics usage, and their hair length and styling. Now change their clothing to a simple shirt and a loose fitting pair of pants. Then remove all their jewelry. Then remove all their eye cosmetics, rouge, and lipstick. Now crop their hair close to the head, and part it on the side. Snapping a picture before and after this make-over will fully demonstrate the part of the minimax principle which states that females act to maximize the differences among themselves, and their differences from males. The lesson here is that the probable reason that females in our culture are treated differently than males is that *they behave differently,* and thank God for that! Most women understand this.

The message to feminists is that *if you want to be treated like a man, you must behave like a man.* That is fundamental.

While many of my open-minded feminist friends—who formerly thought they did not have the same freedoms, rights, and powers as males—will be enlightened by these revelations, and realize that *the ultimate cradle of power is in their hands,* by virtue of their selection of the father of their children, and their dominant influence in the rearing of those children; others will rather have a migraine headache and break into hives than acknowledge the double-standard in the gender grooming data, and that is understandable, for we are always stressed when we are confronted with information that is at odds with our sincerest beliefs, especially when those beliefs are used as an explanation for our frustrations and failures in life, whether real or imagined; and still others will become peevish—traumatized by the thought of giving up their long hair, mascara, lipstick, bare legs, and colorful clothing styles—and will suggest that men are free to exercise the same grooming liberties as females, though at the same time secretly hoping that they do not, dreading the prospect of having to compete not only with their sisters and girlfriends, but with pretty men as well, for the attention and influence that rightfully belongs to them. As for *lesbians*—female homosexuals who are heavily represented in the feminist ranks—they are indeed caught in a society that does not address their needs; but they exacerbate their plight by remaining *covert* and trying to fit into the mold of the *heterosexual grooming dynamic.* The separate agendas of lesbians and heterosexual females cannot be addressed by society until they can be visibly and unequivocally differentiated from each other.

In any case, an expansion of consciousness, while often disconcerting in the short run, is always beneficial to the individual and society in the long term. Next, we will turn our attention to the contrasting dynamics of male behavior vis-à-vis that of the female population, and which represents the other main part of the minimax principle.

4. Minimization of Male Variation

We have seen how females act to maximize their differences. The other half of the minimax principle of gender dynamics observes that males act to *minimize* the differences among themselves.

This dynamic was revealed most dramatically by male hair grooming habits, in which they were found to crop their hair close to the head, often wearing a ritualized part on the left side; also shaving their beards on a daily basis, producing a homogenized look.

Next we saw how males shunned all the cosmetics that females use to make themselves more unique. For example, few males were found to use mascara, rouge, or lipstick to enhance their looks.

Similarly, males were found to use relatively little jewelry, when compared to that worn by females. The jewelry that was worn commonly by men—wristwatches, rings, and necklaces—tended to be of a standard design with little of the variation observed among female versions of these jewelry pieces.

It was in the area of clothing that we saw exactly how little variation there is among men in their behavior. Whereas females were seen to wear a wide variety of clothing styles, males were found to wear garments which varied little in style. The common male suit exemplified this gender dynamic most noticeably, in terms of the similarity of its tailoring and the suit's restriction to the colors of blue, gray, and brown. This in combination with a white shirt and the obligatory necktie was seen to create a virtual male uniform.

Finally, the minimax principle of gender dynamics was crystallized by a comparison of male and female behavior at formal "black-tie" gatherings. Here we saw the often instructive "limiting case," wherein the females attempted to be not only unique from other females, but to be unique from their own former selves, going to great lengths to create an entirely novel look, to be the most fabulous they had ever been at any time and any place.

In contrast, the males at these formal gatherings reached their limiting possibility for minimization of differences, all wearing a uniform tuxedo, in addition to having close cropped hair, a "part," and a clean shaven face—homogenization at its extreme. The polarization of males and females at such formal gatherings is evident when we realize that on the *minimax scale* there are nothing but 0's and 10's in the room.

We can speculate here, and only half in jest, that it is a conspiracy of the female population—whether as mothers, sisters, teachers, or targets of courtship—that achieves *both horns* of the minimax principle, by discriminating among men in subtle ways in order to produce the observed *minimization of male variation,* while at the same time *maximizing and enhancing their own uniqueness.* It seems unlikely that males would consciously and voluntarily act to minimize their differences, while females are maximizing theirs. And since neither the federal government, CIA, nor the KGB is dictating this self-effacing male behavior, what else can we conclude but that it is a well-cloaked female conspiracy, most likely among the many *near-beauties*—rather than the relatively few natural beauties—with the wannabee's having the most to gain from the exaggerated cosmetic efforts that we have been studying.

This conspiracy theory will sound familiar to those die-hard feminists who are still convinced that it is men who possess all the power in contemporary society. Even recently a panel of the most vocal feminists were seen on the TV talk show circuit chanting their ritual incantation about *being on the fringes of society dominated by male cultural hegemony;* one wearing a red dress, one a green dress, one a yellow dress, and one a purple dress; all with bared shaven legs; all wearing long and stylized hair; all wearing earrings, bracelets, and necklaces; and among them, wearing fifteen different shades of mascara, rouge, and lipstick; while the short-haired, blue-suited, face-shaven host commiserated with their sorry plight.

So, unless it is a manifestation of *underlying genetic differences,* as we have posited, it remains an open question as to *who* or *what* is responsible for this marked difference in gender behavior, where males homogenize themselves, while females make themselves unique. It is worth noting, in passing, that the financially huge industries of female hair grooming, cosmetics, jewelry, and clothing, are all dominated in every respect by male *homosexuals,* well in excess of their 10%, or so, incidence in the population at large. A further analysis of this particularly ironic phenomenon is left as an exercise.

After our exhaustive analysis of gender differences in hair grooming, cosmetics usage, jewelry wearing, and clothing preference behavior, there can be no doubt about the validity of the minimax principle of gender dynamics as a comprehensive description of male and female grooming behavior in contemporary Western society. We are not talking about gender differences that are marginal and open to question, but forms of behavior that are visible to anyone who cares to see them.

That many of the forms of behavior that we have observed in Western civilization are not apparent throughout the world, does not distract from their validity, for we know that evolutionary change, whether biological or behavioral, takes time to spread from one place to another. There are still cultures that have not yet learned to read, but that does not invalidate the alphabet. Our interest is in the study of the cutting edge of evolutionary change, and in most instances a study of other less developed cultures will confirm our findings and conclusions to a greater or lesser extent.

Having fully documented the existence of extensive gender differences in behavior, and, most importantly, identified a consistent pattern in those differences, we can now consider the reasons for these differences between males and females.

5. The Biological Basis of Gender Differences

From the very start we set out to compare gender differences in behavior that were clear-cut and not open to debate, for if we could identify dramatic differences between males and females, the inference would follow that less marked differences also exist. These gender differences, in turn, would have implications for all aspects of our civilization; from child-rearing, to education, to legislation, to the workplace, to virtually every societal institution.

We have, in fact, succeeded in clearly identifying many gender differences in behavior, and the observed differences are all the more important because they are not a grab-bag of unrelated conduct with no integrating principle, but rather represent the most basic of behaviors, all related to *mating* dynamics, which in turn dictate the biological and behavioral evolution of contemporary civilization.

Our task now is to take the small logical step from acknowledging these gender differences in mating-related behaviors—hair grooming, cosmetics usage, jewelry wearing, and clothing preference—to the belief that these behavioral differences are *manifestations of underlying genetic differences between males and females.*

It is one thing if behavioral variation is fleeting and due to chance variations in the physical environment, and it is something else entirely if *behavioral differences are due to the unfolding of underlying genetic characteristics.* While science is nowhere near so advanced as to prove conclusively that (say) the wearing of mascara and lipstick is genetically based, in the meantime we can make reasoned arguments for the biological basis of these types of observed gender differences in grooming behavior.

The gender differences in behavior that we have catalogued are so *wide in kind and number,* and so *organized in principle,* and so *resistant to change,* that it should not be difficult to accept the behavior as organically based, especially in the absence of a persuasive counterargument. Just as a female's genetically based skeletal and muscular composition lead her to *walk with a gait unlike that of a male,* we can easily imagine how genetic composition can also dictate differences in other sorts of behavior as well. And we should be less surprised if the genetically based behavioral differences are related to *mating dynamics,* for this is the essence of evolutionary development in all species.

We are assuming, then, based on overwhelming evidence, that gender differences in hair grooming, cosmetics usage, jewelry wearing, and clothing preferences, and the associated minimax principle, are primarily manifestations of underlying genetic differences between males and females. How likely is it, for instance, that the female population would (or could) willingly abandon their unique hair grooming, cosmetics usage, jewelry wearing, and clothing behaviors, to attain a *homogeneous parity with males.* In some segments of the Islamic culture we do, in fact, see the homogenization of women, dictated by religious sanctions, but the jury is still out whether this cultural pressure can override a more basic biological dynamic, which already is rearing its head in many parts of Islam. So again, the exception only proves the rule.

In the following sections we will analyze our observed gender differences in the context of their underlying genetic bases, with emphasis on their evolutionary implications.

6. Female Competition for Desirable Males

We have observed dramatic gender differences in a variety of grooming behaviors. There is no question about the existence of these differences, and little doubt about their genetic origins: the question we must answer with respect to the minimax principle of gender dynamics is why do females act to *maximize* their variation, while males act to *minimize* theirs, *instead of the other way around?*

The balance of the evidence suggests that the motive behind the striking tendency for females, rather than males, to maximize the variation among themselves, is to attract the attentions of a *limited number of desirable male mating partners.* The key concept here is "limited number," for in this respect we honor the common female complaint that there just are not enough good men around. In contrast, we rarely hear men complain about a shortage of desirable women, only the difficulty in attracting them.

This is consistent with our forthcoming analysis, in which we agree that there is indeed only a relatively small number of highly desirable genetically endowed males. In statistical terms this is referred to as a *skewed* population, wherein a relatively few members are outstanding (in a given direction), while the majority are clumped together with minimal differences. Females, on the other hand, are more evenly distributed in their positive qualities, accounting in part for their drive to maximize the differences among themselves in competition for the few prime males, who tend to stand out from the homogenized male population.

The shortage of desirable males—vis-à-vis the number of desirable females—will be more easily understood in the context of gender differences in fertility and *childbearing ability.* In terms of reproductive capacity, males have far greater potential than females. The average female can reproduce, at most, twenty or so children in a lifetime, *regardless of the number of mates she has.* A male, on the other hand, can, in theory, produce a virtually unlimited number of children with multiple mates throughout his entire lifetime.

This genetic difference in the reproductive capacity of males and females, in conjunction with the well-documented fact that offspring tend to possess the characteristics of their parents, leads naturally to the evolution of *polygamous* behavior; wherein the choicest males mate with many females, resulting in the maximum number of choice children. Now the definition of "choice," "select," "prime," or "desirable" males, terms which we have used interchangeably, will vary from species to species. In the sea lion or hippopatamus species, the choicest males might be defined in terms of an optimum combination of quickness and physical size; in another species it might be running speed, or an anatomical correlate of it; in yet another it might be visual acuity, or a behavioral correlate of it; and in yet another species it might be strength or endurance. Over and over again we see species in which the males and females compete among themselves to demonstrate their "desirable" qualities, in order to win the mating opportunities with the most desirable members of the opposite gender, thereby passing on to the next generation the best possible genetic pool.

In the human species the definition of the most desirable males can also vary from one socio-cultural-geographic civilization to another. In the jungles of the Amazon basin, eye-hand coordination or running speed might be best, as evidenced by its success in capturing game. In the severe winter locales, males with muscles to fight grizzly bears and fall trees to build a log cabin may be the choice among females. In modern Southern California, a husky chest might not be as desirable as a husky bank account, as evidenced by a Mercedes Benz parked in the driveway of a twenty-room house, a correlate of the abstracted ability to produce wealth and hence support many children.

We will address this central concept of "desirable" male and female mates more fully in the final chapter. For now, the aspect of the minimax principle to keep in mind is the proposition that the dramatic grooming behavior among females reflects an underlying genetic drive to compete for reproductive opportunities with a limited number of desirable mates.

7. Polygamy as the Natural Human Order

The marked gender differences that we have observed have ramifications for all aspects of human existence, but none is so important as the implication that *polygamy is the natural order among humans as it is in most animal species.*

Although the details may vary from one population to another, the dynamic is the same: the composition of future generations is dependent upon *who mates with whom.* A monogamous population will create a different population from a polygamous population, by virtue of the different parental pairings. As such, the issue of monogamy vs. polygamy is central to the course of development of the human species.

We have found that females maximize their differences in order to compete for a limited number of desirable males. Even in contemporary Western society, where there are *more single males than females* under the reproductive age of forty, women still complain that there are not enough good men. This genetic disparity in the number of desirable males and females leads directly to the conclusion that polygamy, rather than monogamy, is the natural biological drive among humans as it is in the vast majority of animal species.

In comtemporary civilization, much of the observed female grooming behavior and competition for select males is exaggerated, ritualized, and frustrated, for in a monogamous society of one woman for one man, many desirable and talented women will necessarily have to settle for less than desirable mates to father their children.

It is no wonder, then, that when women are fighting among themselves tooth and nail *for a limited number of desirable males,* that a large number of them *will fall short of their aspirations,* and this in turn is reflected in the complete failure of institutionalized monogamy and the *high level of female frustrations and grievances;* from being emotionally unfulfilled, to being physically battered or deserted by their chosen mates, to being driven to aborting their fetuses, to crippling their offspring through an indiscriminate and wholesale use of intoxicants. And this is only the surface of the evil wreaked upon human civilization by institutionalized monogamy.

In the final chapter we will see how the modern practice of institutionalized monogamy—a ritualized vestige of a bygone rural era—is responsible for most of the ills of contemporary urban society, and how polygamy—which has genetic dynamics in its favor—will ultimately prevail and create a better world for all.

8. Heuristic Value of the Minimax Principle

We have discovered that females differ from males in important behavioral ways. We studied only four categories of behavior—hair grooming, cosmetics usage, jewelry wearing, and clothing preferences—and we found consistent and dramatic differences in each instance; which we summarized and synthesized into the *minimax principle of gender dynamics.*

Even without considering the nature of the observed differences, the establishment of gender differences in behavior has wide implications. If marked differences exist in four separate categories of behavior, it immediately follows that there must be scores of other types of behavior which also differentiate between males and females.

These gender differences, in turn, have implications for all aspects of our lives; including childbearing and rearing, education, career choices, governmental policies, physical and psychological healthcare, and virtually every social convention that touches our lives. In this respect the minimax principle will serve the *heuristic* function of generating interest and research in other genuine gender differences, with an aim toward changing societal policies to the better.

It is not our primary purpose here to consider all the other ways in which males and females differ, or the many implications of these differences, for that is a task too large for a single sitting. Rather, our interest is in the most pressing implication; namely, that polygamy is the natural drive among humans just as it is in most of the animal world.

Although this implication of the minimax principle, and related topics, require extensive analysis and discussion by scholars in all disciplines, we will devote the final chapter to a brief outline of some of the more salient aspects of this most important of all contemporary issues.

9. Summary and Conclusions

In this chapter we have reviewed the *minimax principle of gender dynamics,* including its supporting data and its major implications.

We saw how gender differences in grooming behavior were both dramatic and systematic, with females invariably acting to maximize the differences among themselves. In addition to its secondary autoerotic functions, this grooming behavior was seen primarily as a sign of competition among females for a limited number of select males.

The extent and nature of the behavioral gender differences, and the asymmetry in the number of genetically desirable females and males, pointed to a genetic origin of the female competition for male mates; which in turn was seen to be consistent with the presence of a polygamous drive among humans as it is in other animal species.

Whereas various forms of female competitive behavior is functional in a polygamous civilization, it becomes ritualized and aberrant in a monogamous society, where large numbers of females must settle for male mates who can be characterized as less than desirable.

The stress created by the disparity between the genetically based female drive for a desirable male mate to father her children, and the actual result of those efforts, is reflected in the tragically high divorce rate of contemporary monogamous society; the perceived cause of most female grievances and cultural ills as a whole.

In the concluding chapter we will take a closer look at the negative consequences of institutionalized monogamy, and the contrasting and more positive implications of polygamy; conclusions to which we have been ineluctably led by the minimax principle of gender dynamics.

Chapter 7

Evolutionary Implications

1. Introduction

The minimax principle of gender dynamics has provided insights into fundamental behavioral differences between males and females—especially with regard to key mating-related grooming habits—and has forced us to the very important conclusion that the human genetic drive is directed more toward *polygamy* than it is toward monogamy.

Polygamy, a population mating characteristic in which multiple reproductive mates is the norm, is common in a wide variety of animal species. In most species, it is the select males that have multiple female reproductive mates, rather than vice versa. We will see that there are logical reasons for this mating dynamic, based on principles of inheritance and gender differences in childbearing potential.

Among humans, polygamy has been practiced in a wide variety of societies throughout history, and to a lesser extent even today. Although polygamy is widely acknowledged and encouraged in the Judeo-Christian Bible—indeed, representing the very foundation of this religion, wherein pre-eminent males fathered many children from many wives, establishing the genetic pool which continued to inbreed to this very day—revisionist forces have succeeded in suppressing this reality from the public consciousness.

In contemporary culture, the monogamous lifetime mating practice—one female with one male—has supplanted polygamy to such an extent that polygamous behavior has been legislated out of existence and is punishable by imprisonment and social sanction, with tragic consequences for the composition of the world population.

In this concluding chapter we will begin to show the damage being done to modern civilization by the arbitrary institutionalization of monogamy, and by the concomitant suppression of the genetically driven practice of polygamy.

2. Principles of Inheritance

To understand the differences in the consequences to populations formed by the practice of monogamy vs. polygamy, it is necessary to have an overall idea of the principles of inheritance. We do not need to know all the details of genetics, for surely they will not all be known for centuries to come. Also, we do not need to know about the chemical structure and dynamics of DNA, chromosomes, and protein molecules. But we should be familiar with some broad concepts of genetics for which there is wide agreement, and that are sufficient for our purposes.

"Like father, like son." That pretty much sums up the principles of inheritance.

More specifically, children tend to have the same attributes as their parents—both father and mother, as well as grandparents and great grandparents—with the hereditary contribution decreasing the further back in the genealogy that we go.

Certainly our characteristics are not exactly the same as our parents and grandparents, for who can deny that brothers and sisters often differ markedly from one another, and from their parents. Still, siblings are more alike than a random sample of unrelated individuals, and they are more similar to their parents than to their friends' parents. The similarity is *probabilistic* in nature, due to a random sampling of genetic information from both parents, some of which is latent, or recessive, and not apparent in the parents' overt characteristics. That is why great talent sometimes springs out of nowhere, from undistinguished parents; while parents of great accomplishment and ability sometime bear children who are real zeroes. Who has not seen this. But, again, these exceptions only prove the rule that *children tend to be like their parents.*

There is considerable debate about how much of the parent-child similarity is due to inborn genetic factors, and how much is due to learning and interactions with the environment. We will not be drawn into this debate, except to state that the weight of evidence (especially studies of twins separated at birth and reared in independent environments, not to mention casual observation) points to genetics as being of primary importance in shaping human behavior. Mozart composed music by the age of ten that you and I could not hope to create with a hundred years of tutoring. The same is true for all exceptional talent.

Just as the presence of rich soil, rainfall, and sunlight will influence the growth of a plant and its fruit, environmental factors will determine human development; but in each case it is the plant *seed* and human *fertilized egg* that dictates the potential for growth. The variation in genetic possibilities is much wider than the fleeting variation in external environmental factors. That is why owners of race horses pay vast sums of money to breed their horses to other fast race horses, instead of saving money and breeding them to slow horses, hoping to make up the difference with training efforts. Philosophers who continue to debate this age-old *nature vs. nuture* question are perhaps unwilling to resolve it one way or another for fear of being unable to cope with the logical implications, preferring to sit on their hands while the world burns. Our position is squarely in the corner of genetics, not for ideological reasons, but as an acknowledgment of the weight of the empirical data.

So, not only do race horses, dogs, and cats depend on their parents for their attributes, but the same is true in the human realm; tall parents tend to have tall children; musically gifted parents tend to have musically inclined children; mathematically able parents have similarly endowed children. We could go on and on and name hundreds upon hundreds of human characteristics that are passed on from parent to child; but the point to understand is, that although there are exceptions in the extent of a trait passed on from parent to child, there is still a non-random relationship between characteristics of the parents and the children, due to genetics.

The relationship is only approximate since the traits of the mother and father (and grandfather and grandmother, on each parent's side) each influence the child's characteristics. If both parents are tall (or whatever), then the child is more likely to be tall than if just one parent is tall and the other is short. Some characteristics are passed on if *either* parent possesses it, while other traits are passed on only if *both* parents possess it in their genetic library, and still other characteristics are *latent* in a parent's genetic makeup, and may depend on the presence of *other* genetic characteristics for their transmission from one generation to the next. In short, the rules of genetics are complicated in their detail, but simple overall: children tend to inherit the characteristics of their parents. So, there is considerable truth to the adage that *the apple does not fall far from the tree*.

3. Mating Configurations

A true understanding of the simple rule of inheritance—that children tend to possess the characteristics of their parents—has major implications for the future course of civilization.

The nature of the population at any given time is a function of *which females mated with which males, and the number of children born from different types of match-ups.* If this fact is not clear, imagine a population of 100 females and 100 males. Now consider alternative ways in which they might be paired for mating and bearing children. One possibility is to match them based on a lottery drawing, wherein each female is equally likely to be matched up with any of the males. Another possibility is to match them based on height; the tallest female with the tallest male, the second tallest female with the second tallest male, etc. Or perhaps they could be matched on the basis of weight. Or based on the score on some test. Or any of a number of ways.

Potentially, there are literally *millions* of different sets of male-female pairings that are possible from this relatively small population. Now let us imagine that they have been paired in some manner and each couple gives birth to *one* child. The characteristics of these 100 children will depend on how their parents were paired. With a completely different pairing, the characteristics of the 100 offspring would be quite different.

In the above example we assumed each couple would bear only a single child. Now let us consider the consequences of different couples bearing different numbers of children; some only one, some two, some three, and so on. Clearly, the characteristics of the total child population will be slanted in the direction of *the traits of those parents who had the greater number of children.*

We see, then, that the three most important things that determine the characteristics of our population are (1) parental characteristics, (2) the dynamics that determine who mates with whom, and (3) the relationship between parental characteristics and their frequency of childbearing. Also important, of course, is how the children are raised by the parents, but this potential is subsumed under the first factor, parental characteristics.

In the initial example above we assumed that each of the 100 males in our hypothetical population mated and bore one child with just one female—a monogamous arrangement. Now let us contrast the result of that type of arrangement with a polygamous one in which, say, 20 of the 100 males mated and had a child with *three* females each, accounting for 60 of the 100 children; and let us further assume that the remaining 80 men had sexual intercourse with the remaining 40 women, yielding the remaining 40 children—noting that only 40 of these 80 males would actually be the *genetic* fathers of these 40 children.

So, in the above examples, each of the 100 females each gave birth to a single child, *whether in the monogamous or polygamous scenario;* the key difference between the monogamous and polygamous arrangements being in terms of which *males* were the hereditary fathers, and consequently were represented in the genetic pool of the 100 children. Two things are clear. Firstly, the population of 100 children born of the monogamous arrangement are different, in total, from the 100 children born of the polygamous arrangement, by virtue of the different set of males fathering the children. Secondly, the nature of the child population from the polygamous arrangement will depend largely upon *which of the males mated with multiple females.*

With these fundamental understandings in mind, let us move on to a further analysis of gender differences to gain a deeper insight into the dynamics of alternative mating arrangements and their consequences for the genetic composition of the population.

4. Gender Differences in Childbearing Potential

At most, females can bear twenty or so children in a lifetime. Males, in sharp contrast, can theoretically bear hundreds of children, by mating with different females throughout their entire lifetimes.

This genetic difference between males and females in childbearing potential is of no consequence in monogamous populations, but it is of supreme importance in the development of polygamous populations.

In the monogamous population, by definition, the male can only father as many children as the mother can bear, and his childbearing years are prematurely over when his wife reaches menopause. Consequently, the male genetic potential for fathering a very large number of children can only be actualized in a polygamous population.

In contrast to the male, the female's childbearing potential is the same whether in a monogamous or polygamous society. In either case she can bear at most twenty or so children. The only distinction is that in a monogamous population all her children will be fathered by the same male. In a polygamous population, her children could possibly be fathered either by a single male or different males. But the *number* of children she can bear remains the same.

Here we begin to see more than an inkling of a real *genetic rationale* for the *minimax principle of gender dynamics*. Since females are limited in the number of children they can bear, they will be highly motivated to compete with other females for the opportunity to mate with the most desirable males—rather than with the *dregs* of the population—to assure that the quality of their children is among the best. With a polygamous population dynamic, a woman's investment in hair grooming, cosmetics usage, jewelry wearing, and clothing choices—to set herself apart from her sisters and other females—will more likely pay off than in the monogamous scenario of today, where most females necessarily have to settle for the *schmo's* of society; and have nothing but frustrations and grievances as a consequence of their ritualized grooming efforts, not to mention the dubious characteristics of their children.

Given the gender differences in childbearing potential, the associated differences in grooming behavior, and polygamy as the natural human dynamic, we will look next at the particular attributes that make males and females desirable to one another for purposes of mating.

5. Parental Characteristics

Mating between males and females in not indiscriminate. Certain features of prospective mates are more appealing than others. Despite the difficulty in providing an exhaustive definition of what attracts people to one another, we know from experience that males and females are often attracted to each other in an instant—*love at first sight*—as if we have a personal template in our head that can instantaneously sort through the many dimensions upon which we all vary, and acts as a gateway to our heart.

We have repeatedly used terms such as *desirable, good, prime, choice, top, select, best, finest, elite, good, superior, greatest,* etc. to describe the type of males for whom females are competing, and similarly, the types of females sought by males.

While the meaning of this "desirability" concept is understood intuitively, it cannot be defined in a *noncircular* way; that is, the words we have available to define it need defining themselves, and in the end, their definitions are found to depend on the very concept they are trying to define.

As such, it is a very basic concept in human affairs. These types of concepts, which cannot be defined in noncircular language, and usually require *pointing* operations and *examples* for their definition, are often referred to as *primitive* concepts. Other examples include the notion of a point in geometry; the statistical concept of probability; the directions left, right, up, and down; basic tastes such as salty or sweet; feelings of pain and pleasure; beauty; and various colors; to name a few such primitive concepts.

While ideas such as a geometrical point, statistical probability, or subatomic particles, remain abstract analytical concepts; notions such as salty, painful, stinky, loud, beautiful, and blue require definition through their sensation. Although we might define the color blue, for instance, as the color of the sky, we are still dependent on someone to point to the sky to let us know what the sky is in the first place, and then other blue objects must be pointed out until we discriminate the color from the object.

In terms of gender dynamics the concept of *desirability* has the added complication that what is desirable in a female is not exactly the same as what is desirable in a male. We have seen this in our study of the minimax principle, where females were found to groom themselves not only to maximize the differences among themselves—to make themselves more unique—but also to distance themselves from the typical male appearance.

If we want to fully understand mating dynamics and to evaluate the relative merits of a monogamous vs. polygamous society, we need to understand which characteristics make a female desirable to a male, and vice versa.

From the start we have to admit that there is no one identifiable characteristic among either males or females that defines mating desirability. If we had to name a single gender-related characteristic that defines desirability, we would be forced to name *beauty* among females and *wealth* among males. But money alone is not the sole determinant of what females pursue in a male, otherwise the fraudulent banker or stock manipulator who steals family savings; or the pornographer who demeans the human spirit; or the purveyors of gambling, whiskey, and tobacco, who cause the misery and deaths of millions of people; or the distributors of addictive drugs who lead mothers to toss their babies into the dumpster, would be as universally desirable as those men who accumulate their wealth by expanding the human potential and contributing to the lasting joyfulness in the world.

So, desirability cannot be nailed down as a single characteristic, independent of other considerations. Rather, it is an entire *constellation* of biological and behavioral characteristics, but beauty is often its hallmark, so it deserves special attention vis-à-vis other traits.

6. Beauty, Brains, Muscles, and Money

Beauty—one of those fundamental concepts that requires actual examples for its ultimate definition—is certainly important for both females and males. However, it is more important among females than it is among males. We have seen this in our study of the *minimax principle,* wherein females are driven to enhance their beauty through hair grooming, cosmetics usage, jewelry wearing, and clothing behavior; making themselves more unique and maximizing the differences among themselves, as well as maximizing their differences from males.

In all instances the female grooming effort was seen to be directed toward mimicking natural standards of beauty defined in terms of consensual aesthetic judgments; more specifically, to look like the females in the advertisements for personal grooming products. In this context we can again see the intrinsic appeal of female *breasts* as a measure of beauty in the eyes of males, for ample breasts—through evolution—are correlated with the ability to raise viable children. Indeed, their appeal often competes with facial beauty, as evidenced by the large number of magazines and movies (recent technological innovations) which appeal to broad segments of the male population by featuring females displaying their bare breasts and buttocks; but who in other respects are homely or nondescript at best, and by their postures and the vile or presumptuous look in their eyes do not always represent the type of woman you would want as the mother of your children.

So breasts alone cannot compete with a pretty face. Despite the inherent attractiveness of female breasts and buttocks, the ultimate criterion of beauty remains in the *face;* for it varies on so many dimensions, and offers so many more communicative possibilities than any other feature of the human anatomy, and in its high visibility submits to evolutionary development toward an even greater ideal.

Among males, in contrast, the ability to generate *wealth* is perhaps the most desirable characteristic to females, for this not only enhances her stature and adds to the comfort of her life, but it assures that her children will be fed, sheltered, and prepared for a productive life.

In comparison to readily apparent wealth, the more limited appeal of "brains" is due to the fact that they are hidden under the skull and therefore invisible to the naked eye. Many individuals claim to have them, but few present the proof. Indeed, we as a civilization have difficulty defining the necessary *evidence* for the presence of a functioning brain, or *intelligence* as we are wont to call it. In fact, Western society has skirted the issue by defining it as *the capacity to do well in school.* But clearly this is a circular definition, for as our school curriculum changes, so too must our definition of intelligence, and vice versa. This type of thinking only begs the question as to what we should teach in our schools.

Somewhere we must make a distinction between *intelligence* and the ability to accumulate *wealth,* but this is not a simple task and cannot be done in a single paragraph. Intelligence is a *multivariate* trait, and there are probably as many types of specific intelligence as there are job listings in the newspaper. Some individuals have more abilities than others, but there is no one thing as intelligence per se, unless it is the *weighted combination* of separate aptitudes; but then we are faced with the intractable task of having to identify and place *meaningful values* on those separate traits, values which could well differ from one culture to another, and from one era to another. Ultimately, though, I think we need to define the highest form of intelligence as the ability to identify and solve societal problems, and to contribute to the lasting joy of the world. Very often this also creates wealth, and rightfully so, for such individuals should be afforded the opportunities to raise many children who will carry their desirable traits to the next generation. But conversely, we as a society must be suspicious about wealth-producing activities that do not create a better world, but rather capitalize on, and perpetuate, our weaknesses—especially with regard to the sure profits to be gained from the universal activities centering on unfulfilled sexual desire, gambling, and intoxicants. In a sane society, the risk-free profits to be reaped from filling these everpresent reflexive needs—*our unsuppressable societal vices*—is the province of the *government,* and not the criminal underworld or anti-societal entrepreneurs, who through regressive laws are given license to collect these sure profits at inflated levels for their own benefit. In the hands of the government, as proxy for the public, such profits—whether through heavy taxation or *outright administration of the vices*—revert back to the good of society, rather than furnishing the mansions of selected individuals. There are also degrees of wealth obtained through sundry forms of theft, scams, extortion, graft, gouging, and various other non-productive activities. In the end, it is the responsibility of the *truly beautiful females* of society to distinguish these types of exploitive and degenerative wealth from the productive forms, in order that they can deny mating opportunities to these anti-societal individuals (as well as their lawyers and accountants), forcing them to marry *ugly scags,* so that their offspring for generations to come will be quickly recognized by their repugnant looks, providing a basis for their eventual elimination from society that will be more effective than any laws or prison bars. Finally, it is left as an exercise to contrast the desirability of *earned* wealth vs. *inherited* wealth, in an evolutionary and mating perspective.

So while the notion of *beauty* is something that everyone can agree upon, the nature and quality of *wealth* and *intelligence* are not so clearly recognized at first glance. Fortunately, one aspect of intelligence is the ability to recognize it in others, so we are assured at least some degree of correlation between the attributes of mothers and fathers. In this respect, an important area of research is to identify readily visible characteristics that are correlates of intelligence or future productivity.

Related to the importance of wealth and intelligence is the carryover appeal of *muscles* in men, for in an evolutionary perspective a muscular build was associated with success in building a shelter, capturing game, and fighting off foes. In this evolutionary respect, muscles are the male analog of female breasts, both related to the viability of their offspring. Note, in this context, how females enter beauty contests with emphasis on their breasts, while males enter sports contests of strength, speed, and endurance. Note, too, that there is a sufficient size for both female breasts and male muscles, with breasts and muscles of an exaggerated size having only limited appeal. Also, we have already noted that a big wallet is often more appealing than big muscles in this modern age, as the evolutionary value of physical strength begins to dissipate in favor of abstracted intellectual labor that generates money to buy the services originally requiring big biceps. But men, save your barbells—a muscular male physique will still be in favor among females for a long time to come, for the evolutionary work of millennia is not undone overnight. Chess championships have not yet caught the imagination of the valley girl.

Male buttocks, incidentally, are attractive to females, just as female buttocks are attractive to males. But there is a difference in the nature of the appeal. While males prefer a rounded female derriere in fair proportion to the breasts, separated by a narrow waist, forming an *hour-glass* figure; females prefer a more compact butt among males, one that is small and "cute" relative to the broader chest and shoulders, forming a *V-shaped* figure. These contrasting gender standards of beauty are again related to the evolutionary dynamics of viable child rearing: The female hour-glass figure emphasizes both the child*bearing* capacity of *broad hips,* and the child *rearing* capacity of *ample breasts;* while the V-shaped male figure, established by a relatively small butt, emphasizes the *broader chest and shoulders* as the crucial features of strength needed for assuring a viable family, in an evolutionary perspective.

Not coincidentally, the males who have accumulated wealth, or who have the potential to do so, also tend to be above average in beauty. This beauty has been inherited primarily from the *mother,* since the best wealth producers tend to mate with the most beautiful females, other things equal. When is the last time you saw an ugly girl in a sports car? It is easy to see, then, that the wealthy male has gained his production skills primarily from his father, and his beauty mainly from his mother. In this type of recursive evolution from generation to generation, the *confluence of beauty and wealth* becomes established.

This association between beauty and wealth is stronger in the polygamous society than it is in the monogamous one. Indeed, *monogamy militates against both the evolution of beauty and the potential to create wealth,* and even more so against the joint occurrence of beauty and wealth; primarily because so many low desirability males father so many children in a monogamous society vis-à-vis that in a polygamous one. To fully understand this dynamic, refer back to our earlier discussion of the hypothetical population of 100 males and 100 females, first mating according to the rules of monogamy and then according to the rules of polygamy. In the ritualized monogamous society, many average females are forced to mate with non-productive and less than attractive lower echelon males, resulting in children with neither beauty nor productive abilities. Can we really blame these women for aborting their worthless children?

We can see now why males and females differ in the nature of their desirable characteristics. In broad strokes, the main business of life is the reproduction of desirable children and the production of a better world for them: the female's key role in this equation is to *reproduce,* while the male's key role is to *produce.* Since the female can pass on her genetic characteristics to at most twenty or so children, while the male can pass his on to hundreds, the ability to produce (wealth, knowledge, joy) evolves primarily as a male trait in a polygamous population; the historic origins of the human species.

Since all women have essentially the same childbearing potential, and since the producer function rests mainly with a small group of males—and cannot be feigned by either males or females—the main way for most females to get a leg up on her competition for mating opportunities with the choice male producers is to make herself more beautiful, other things equal. This has been well-documented with the *minimax principle of gender dynamics,* where it was found that females unilaterally act to maximize the differences among themselves, while emulating accepted standards of beauty.

In a polygamous population it makes sense for females to invest great amounts of time and effort in competition for the most desirable males, for many of them will succeed, by virtue of their sharing the prime males. In contrast, exaggerated female grooming behavior is not very functional in a monogamous society, which dictates one woman for one man. If virtually every woman is assured a male mate, then there is really no need to go to such extremes of grooming behavior in order to attract a male—there is one for everybody—and the chances of mating with one of the relatively rare desirable males are slim.

As a result, in the monogamous society, many females have to settle for less than highly desirable males, and this is evident from the large number of contemporary female grievances, ranging from emotional neglect, to batterings and beatings, to desertion, to children who are variously delinquents, ingrates, illiterates, or, at best, brats; traits inherited from their fathers, who, in a polygamous society, would not be bearing as many children, due to their negative qualities. But with institutionalized monogamy, this is the price women are willing to pay to have "a man of their own," as it were.

In a later section we will return to the notion of beauty, to more thoroughly study the dynamics of its evolution. For now, we should keep in mind its importance among the female population in determining mating probabilities.

7. Population Dynamics

Earlier we considered a hypothetical population of 100 males and 100 females. Since each female could possibly pair with each of the 100 males, and vice versa, we found that there were millions of different *sets* of monogamous male-female matings that were possible. In larger populations, and in polygamous populations, the number of possibilities accelerates exponentially.

Without having stated it, we assumed the obvious that the 100 females and 100 males in our sample population differed among themselves in any number of variable characteristics, some trivial and some extremely important. It follows, then, that the nature of the child population born in this universe will depend upon *which females mate with which males.*

The desirable characteristics of an exclusively monogamous population will be optimized when the male-female mating configuration follows a strict *hierarchical* or pecking order; that is, when the most desirable females mate with the most desirable males, and the least desirable females mate with the least desirable males, where desirability is defined as an overall, bottomline measure; consisting of a weighted combination of beauty, wealth, brains, and every other characteristic that we consciously or unconsciously take into account in judging the value of a mate.

The nature of the resulting child population will depend upon how closely the desirability hierarchies of the males and females are matched. The following exercises will demonstrate the implications for the child population in monogamous societies; depending upon whether the pecking orders are matched perfectly vs. loosely vs. a completely random matching.

First, let us consider a monogamous population in which there is a *perfect matching* in the desirability levels of the males and females. For our purposes we will consider a simplified population of five males and five females, and, for exposition purposes alone, assign the males and females in each set desirability values of 10, 9, 8, 7, and 6. With a perfect matching of fathers and mothers, we have:

Father values: 10 9 8 7 6
Mother values: 10 9 8 7 6

Next we will make the reasonable assumption that these five couples will bear a child with an expected desirability value equal to the average of their parents' values, and we have:

Child values: 10 9 8 7 6

We see that the *expected values* of the child population duplicates that of the parent population, with both the same *average* value and *variance* of those values.

At first glance it would seem that this ideal monogamous situation, with the perfect matching of parents, would result in stable population values, generation after generation. But there is a crucial wrinkle in the rules of genetics that change the outlook; namely, there is *random variation around the expected value*. That is, children from a particular parental pairing will vary about the expected value. So, while 10-valued parents will—on average—bear 10-valued children, they will also occasionally bear 11-valued and 9-valued children, and, less frequently, other values; remembering, of course, that we are using arbitrary numbers for expositional purposes. Now just as 10-valued parents will occasionally bear 11- or 9-valued children, the 6-valued parents will occasionally bear 7-valued and 5-valued children.

So, after one generation, the distribution of desirability values will have changed from a range of 6 to 10, to one of 5 to 11, or even 4 to 12. Despite this increase in variation, the average of the population has remained the same, assuming all couples have the *same* number of children. We should also keep in mind that in real populations, the sets of parental desirabilities are not likely to be uniformly distributed as in our example, and the distribution of males, as often cited before, is likely to differ from that of females. Still, the essence of the argument is unaffected by these simplifying liberties in the assumptions.

The above set of male-female pairings is just one of many possibilities. Consider that any of 5 females could mate with the first listed male, leaving any of 4 females who could mate with the second male, leaving any of 3 females to mate with the third male, and so on; resulting in $5 \times 4 \times 3 \times 2 \times 1 = 120$ different *sets* of pairings. We can look at some of the more enlightening possibilities.

Let us see what happens to the monogamous population when there is a *negative correlation* between the desirability values of the mothers and fathers; i.e., when *high* desirability values mate with *low* desirability values. Rematching our original parents we have:

Father values: 10   9   8   7   6
Mother values: 6   7   8   9   10

As before, we reasonably assume that the expected values of the children of these pairings will equal the average of their parents' values, and we have:

Child values: 8   8   8   8   8

Notice what has happened. While the *average* desirability value of the new generation has not changed, still 8 as it was before, the *variation* in expected values has disappeared: everyone is the same. But, in fact, as before, there will still be *some variation,* since there will be variation about the value of 8, with a few 9's and 7's, and even fewer 10's and 6's. Still, the most dramatic result of this type of monogamous mating dynamic—where there is a negative relationship between the values of mating partners—is a virtual *homogenization* of the population.

Now let us study the more realistic intermediate ground— neither the ideal perfect pairing first considered, nor the above negative pairing situation, nor a completely random one, but one in which there is an *approximate* pairing of males and females in terms of desirability values. Rematching the males and females in an approximate way, we have:

Father values: 10   9   8   7   6
Mother values: 9   10   8   6   7

Again taking the averages of the respective parental values, the expected values of the children are as follows:

Child values: 9.5   9.5   8   6.5   6.5

We see that this generation of children is not so homogeneous as when there is a negative pairing of parents, but neither is it as varied as the ideal perfect pairing of parental values. While the average value remains at 8, as in every other scenario, there has still been a *homogenization* of the population, with the curtailment of the extreme values. The above example is relatively close to the ideal perfect pairing first discussed; it is left as an exercise to determine the consequences of an even more approximate pairing of parental desirability values, as it approaches a completely *random* pairing of males and females.

The important conclusion to be remembered from the above examples, is that in an exclusively *monogamous* population, a less than perfect pairing of parents in terms of desirability will result in a successive *homogenization* of the population from one generation to the next. Secondly, the average value of the population will remain the same only when all types of parental pairings have the *same* number of children. If, say, the lower valued parents have more children than the higher valued couples, the average of the population will drift lower from one generation to the next. It is left as an exercise to determine what happens to the shape, variance, and average of the population distribution from generation to generation—under the latter conditions.

Now that we have an idea of the negative dynamics of an exclusively monogamous population, we can compare it with the consequences of *polygamous* parenting. For direct comparison with the above examples, let us again assume five children from the same five mothers, but now let us see the result when three of the children have the *same father:*

Father values:	10	10	10	8	6
Mother values:	10	9	8	7	6

In the above example, the three 10's on the father line all represent the *same father,* while the 8 and 6 represent a random selection from the remaining 9-, 8-, 7-, and 6-valued males used in our previous examples. The expected values of the children from this polygamous population will be as follows:

Child values:	10	9.5	9	7.5	6

Compared to the children of the monogamous populations, even the ideal one, we immediately note that with polygamous parenting there are considerably *more high-valued children.* While the range of values is the same, *the average expected value in the polygamous population has increased dramatically.* With this greater incidence of high-valued children—and as before there will be some 11's and 5's among them—the average expected value of *successive* generations will drift even higher. In this example we have chosen a simplified and arbitrary 60:20 female to male mating ratio among the high desirability population members, and a 40:80 female to male ratio among the remaining population, strictly for expositional purposes. In reality, males and females in a polygamous population are likely to vary widely in the number of mates, and consequently their family sizes, but the above example adequately demonstrates the essential difference between polygamous and monogamous population dynamics.

With so many children in a polygamous population born from a relatively small pool of elite fathers, the possibility of inbreeding and its sometimes negative genetic consequences becomes more likely, and it is no doubt for this reason that children came to bear their father's name, rather than their mother's, to signify a common heredity. In a monogamous society, by contrast, where individual males and females contribute equally to the population genetic pool, the assignment of the father's name to the children is totally arbitrary.

While our treatment of population mating dynamics has been necessarily simplified and to a large extent abstract, the essential difference between the evolutionary consequences of monogamous and polygamous populations has been captured. Computer simulations by bio-mathematicians will document our main conclusions, as well as the consequences of various boundary conditions and a variety of secondary assumptions which are beyond the scope of this presentation.

Herein, incidentally, lies the flaw of the Marxist philosophical wish that there can ever be a classless society. The Communist experiment, founded with an ignorance of biology, has barely lasted a century before landing on the scrapheap of bogus ideas. The world cannot be improved by armed revolution alone, but requires the mating of beauty and ability in the context of a polygamous culture recognizing genetic differences.

In the following sections we will shift from the theoretical to the empirical, as we look more closely at some of the more tangible negative consequences of monogamy, which will provide greater meaning and salience to the analysis presented above.

8. The Failures of Monogamy

One cannot help but wonder, why hundreds and thousands of years ago, when the world population was tiny—almost negligible compared to what it is today—that there were so many truly outstanding figures and accomplishments in the arts and sciences; and yet in this modern age, there are relatively so few. This is all the more baffling when one realizes that there are nearly as many people living on the globe at this moment, as previously lived in the past several centuries; and many more than lived during the productive Greek and Roman civilizations millennia ago.

In fact, our preceding analysis of population dynamics points to institutionalized *monogamy*—and the concomitant suppression of polygamy—as the prime cause of the *de-evolution* of the population's desirable characteristics. We discovered that monogamy—actual, as opposed to theoretical—tends to decrease the variation in the population with respect to all genetic characteristics related to mating behavior, so that extremes in either direction are less likely to occur in successive generations. And this is the result when there is no bias in childbearing frequency vis-à-vis parental characteristics. When the least desirable parents bear more children than the most desirable parents, the average of the population actually *deteriorates* from one generation to the next.

How else can we account for the typical student's inability to write a declarative sentence, or follow a logical proof containing more than three steps. With a few exceptions, then, it is no surprise that among *adult* standards of achievement, we find

peurile scribbling masquerading as literature; the vacuous, biz-
zare, and repulsive, alternating as monuments of modern art;
greed run amok in the business world; fetishistic timidity in
government; and in science, the establishment of rigid disci-
plinary boundaries—and boundaries within those boundaries—
serving to protect from outside view the pursuit of the trivial,
while at the same time guarding against contributions from
neighboring colleagues; none of which is a sin in itself, but
then neither are they virtues worthy of a progressive society.

Indeed, most of the ills of contemporary Western civilization can be traced to the institutionalization of monogamy and
the associated prohibition of polygamy, which have resulted in
a de-evolution of both the human spirit and its *genetic foundations.* Although monogamy may have been an expedient in bygone rural societies, its ritualization in modern industrialized
urban civilization has little to recommend it, except that it provides a steady audience for the vulgar soap opera industry.

The problem is not so much with monogamy itself, for
surely it is the desirable arrangement for some individuals, but
the real problem is with *ritualized* monogamy; which blindly
dictates and expects marriage on the basis of one woman to one
man (of the same approximate age), to the exclusion of polygamous mating arrangements. The evolutionary implications
of this arrangement for the composition of the population are
devastating.

We have already seen how the practice of monogamy—one
female reproductive mate for each male—results in a stagna-
tion and constriction in the growth of desirable population
characteristics vis-à-vis that created by polygamy, which is expansive in terms of the propagation of positive population characteristics. In this concluding chapter we have license to
speculate that ritualized monogamy is also responsible for an

exaggerated form of the minimax principle of gender dynamics, where the *inborn* traits of females are masked by cosmetic grooming, while those of males are masked by pressures toward homogenization. In both instances, *the masking of inborn characteristics serves to militate against their potency in evolutionary mating dynamics,* and consequently adversely affects the generational development of positive genetic traits.

The societal institutionalization of monogamy also results in a forced increase in the *homosexual* population; a population which that same society is unprepared to accept in an nondiscriminating manner. While there are still some who doubt that homosexuality is an inborn trait, the amount of evidence in favor of this interpretation is overwhelming. For those who do not live in New York, San Francisco, London, Paris, Tokyo, or other large urban areas with high concentrations of homosexuals, and therefore cannot spot their visible biologically based differences, one need only study the archives of the TV talk shows, where panel after panel of homosexuals assert, in no uncertain terms, that their homosexual character was evident to them from their earliest memory. There is no reason to doubt these self-reports. Ritualized monogamy, where every female is supposed to mate with a male, and vice versa, results in homosexuals marrying the opposite gender and passing on their genetic trait to their children, either in *manifest* or *recessive* form. This type of reproductive mating behavior between homosexuals and heterosexuals would be highly unlikely in a sane and less ritualized society, which would allow homosexuals to overtly signal their sexual affinity and avoid the often tragic pairings of unknowing heterosexuals with *covert* homosexuals. In a ritualized monogamous society where everyone is expected to marry, and where, say, 10% of males and females are homosexual, then it is probable that *nearly 20% of all marriages have at least one homosexual partner.* If this is not a key source of marital discord and emotional trauma, then what is. And who can estimate the consequences for the population genetic pool, when this enforced matrimony among homosexuals continues generation after generation.

But ritualized monogamy has struck its severest blow against the *heterosexual male population,* both in terms of its restrictions on the mating potential of prime males and the homogenization of the male population as a whole. When individual differences between males are masked or suppressed, there is no opportunity for positive traits to have an *edge* over negative traits in terms of evolutionary propagation from one generation to the next. Instead, these positive characteristics are attenuated in successive generations, to a mediocre middle ground, resulting in the *wimpification* of the population. How else can we account for the lack of moral, social, and political leadership in the world today. What scientist, educator, or public figure is willing to voice an unpopular view these days. And where is the media that allows such views?

More immediately, the complete failure of monogamy is best documented by the high incidence of marriages that dissolve in *divorce.* With half of all marriages ending in divorce court, it is not hard to extrapolate that many more marriages are sustained only by economic, social, psychological, or religious sanctions. It is worth noting, again, that whereas in general males ask females to marry, females ask males to divorce.

The minimax principle of gender dynamics has shown us how the competition among females for the small number of select males has resulted in exaggerated and ritualized forms of hair grooming, cosmetics usage, jewelry wearing, and clothing choices. Males, on the other hand, have become homogenized in appearance, and the natural genetic tendency of prime males to have multiple mates, and bear many children throughout life, has been frustrated by the strictures of monogamy. Instead, the least desirable males in society are the ones bearing the most children. Consequently, men are homogenized not only in their physical appearance, but in their child-bearing capabilities as well. This extreme *homogenization* of males in our monogamous society—both in terms of the masking of individual differences and the curtailment of differential childbearing potential—inevitably results in a de-evolution of desirable population characteristics.

The negative consequences of monogamy are also seen in the great number of *grievances* among females. We have already noted the high incidence of divorce, which is a global indication of the dissatisfaction of females with the mates that they themselves had chosen. In the polygamous society, with more females able to live and mate with the *choicest males,* the number of *emotionally satisified* females increases exponentially. Dissatisfied females in such a society can easily move to another family group without suffering the economic and personal hardships associated with monogamous divorce. So there is no such thing as children without fathers in a polygamous society.

And the extent to which females are *battered, beaten, or sexually terrorized* by their husbands in monogamous relationships, is a phenomenon largely unknown in the polygamous society. The freedom of females to move from one family to another makes such cruelty easy to escape, should it exist in the first place. Also, such behavior is only likely to occur among the dregs of the society, who in any case are rapidly bred out of existence by the polygamous mating dynamic, which naturally denies them reproductive mates who would propagate their negative traits to the next generation.

Child abuse is also something that is foreign in the polygamous family, since the majority of children are born in families headed by the choicest males who have mated with the choicest females. Remember that children possess the qualities of their parents. Unloved, runaway children, should they exist, always have another family to join.

Career opportunities for females in the polygamous society are also more likely to develop, both because of the financial resources of the male family head and the child-rearing and housekeeping assistance provided by the other females in the family complex. Very often the family itself becomes a self-sufficient economic entity, by virtue of the variety of talents under the same roof.

We see, then, that in the preferred form of polygamy—where the most desirable males mate with a broad base of the most desirable females, and father many more children than the less desirable males—the population drifts in a positive direction, genetically and behaviorally, so that both the number of exceptional children and the average of the population as a whole, is enhanced from one generation to the next with respect to desirable characteristics: The extreme wealth of the prime males in the polygamous society is devoted to the raising of good children, rather than being invested in gold faucets and ivory statues.

In marked contrast, institutionalized monogamy has a negative effect both on the genetic development of the population and the behavior it engenders, as evidenced by the large number of societal ills growing from its ritualized practice. There are few, if any, advantages that monogamy holds over polygamy. And this is no surprise, for both the minimax principle of gender dynamics and the laws of inheritance have shown us that polygamy is very likely to be a *basic human drive* just as it is among most animal species. Consequently, we should expect ritualized monogamy to soon fall on its face, from its own weight. Fooling with genetic drives never succeeds. *The laws of nature nap, but they do not die.*

9. The Evolution of Beauty

It is not our purpose here to list all of the hundreds upon hundreds of desirable human characteristics besides beauty. Rather, our purpose is to show how *beauty*—which by definition is intrinsically attractive to us—has come to be a visible correlate, or signal, of these other important traits, which are often not so visible at a single glance. Who can tell a person's wit by eye alone?

It makes sense that, other things equal, each of us wants to mate with someone who is beautiful in our eyes. The importance of beauty in the dynamics of mating will become more apparent when we analyze the meaning of "other things equal." Suppose you are faced with choosing between two potential mates who are exactly alike in all respects except beauty. Your choice is predictable.

Now two individuals never have exactly the same set of traits, differing only in beauty, so this hypothetical situation is only meant to represent a limiting and instructive case. More often, two individuals are very close in their remaining traits, and then beauty becomes a kind of tiebreaker, as it were. That is why females believe that every single hair counts; a single hair out of place can make the difference between success and failure in attracting a desirable mate.

Charles Darwin in his *Origin of Species* was the first to document this evolutionary concept of infinitesimal differences in the context of predator-prey relations, observing that although hair-breadth escapes between, say, rabbit and fox, are rare, they most certainly *do occur;* affecting future *mating configurations,* and in the vast crucible of time can accumulate to produce variations in the anatomy and behavior of species from one generation to the next.

We see, then, why the *minimax principle of gender dynamics* makes so much sense in an evolutionary perspective. Given that a female varies minimally, perhaps imperceptibly, from others, she acts to make herself more unique by making herself more beautiful, tipping the scales in her favor in her competition for a desirable male. The enhancement of her beauty is her main recourse, because most other important traits are usually (1) inborn, (2) relatively immutable, and (3) invisible to the casual observer. She cannot carry her resume, vita, or list of talents on her sleeve, but she can use mascara on her eyes, rouge on her cheeks, and polish on her nails.

Here, now, we have to make a distinction between *natural* and *cosmetic* beauty, in terms of their implications for the evolutionary development of the species. If the *near-beauties* are successful in imitating the *natural beauties,* they will indeed mate with desirable males as intended, but the laws of inheritance draw a line here, in that instances of cosmetic beauty (say, thick eyelashes by virtue of mascara) are *not* passed on to the next generation! Rather, the children will inherit the underlying dowdy looks. Thus, cosmetic subterfuges—especially such things as orthodontic braces, nosejobs, facelifts, breast implants, and other practices too gross to even discuss—tend to militate against the evolution of *true beauty.* Pity the children of the poor man who marries the bleached blond with capped teeth, facial surgery, breast implants, and a mail-order diploma. Indeed, this man has every right to sue for breach of promise.

So, while natural characteristics such as wavy hair, rosy cheeks, and attractive eyes can be passed on to our children, their imitative counterparts cannot. Here, then, is the danger of too much cosmetic behavior, for if true differences in beauty are *masked from visibility,* they will not be differentially correlated with the successful mating with desirable males, and therefore will be less likely to be differentially propagated to the next generation in conjunction with the desirable traits of the choice male. Recall the analysis of the evolutionary and stylized development (or lack of it) of relatively invisible armpit and pubic hair vs. the highly visible head hair, eyebrows, or facial beard.

If, however, desirable males are able to discriminate between true beauties and the near-beauties, future generations will not only be more desirable in a productive sense, but also more beautiful as well. The boys from such a mating grow up with the productivity traits of their father and the beauty of their mother (as well as her productivity traits). When the boys become adult males, they too will be desirable as their fathers had been before them, and will have gained an additional edge of beauty. So too with the girls from this mating; they will have inherited their mother's beauty and their father's productivity traits. In this way, beauty and intelligence are wed.

And so it is not peculiar or superficial for males or females to be attracted to beauty, for through evolutionary dynamics it has come to be an easily visible correlate of productivity; certainly not a perfect correlation, God knows, but we have hundreds of generations ahead of us for the work to be done.

If monogamy militates against the generational growth of desirable traits, as outlined above, and if over-zealous cosmetic behavior among females does the same, then we can well imagine the consequences of the two working in conjunction: de-evolution of the human species, with survival of the mediocre and tasteless. How else can we account for the vulgarities of-Hollywood, the bilge of the press, and the popularity of heavy metal music.

10. Old Age in a New Age

One of the most negative consequences of institutionalized monogamy centers on the issue of *age*. In its most ritualized form, monogamy in Western society not only dictates that every female marries a male, preferably sooner than later, but the marriage should be with someone of the same age.

As a result, teen-agers mate with teen-agers, and twenty-year-olds mate with twenty-year-olds. There are devastating consequences for the population of children resulting from this practice. What twenty-year-old male is capable of understanding, much less fulfilling, a woman's emotional needs, either before or after motherhood; and how can such a young male cope with the responsibilities of fatherhood, when he himself still has so much to learn and experience.

Even more importantly, at such a young age there is little basis on which a female can identify a prime male as a prospective father of her children. Most often, men do not show their true potential until later in life, and some are really "late-bloomers" and do not show their talents until they are in their forties, fifties or sixties. Also, while it is often difficult to identify talent in youth, age has the advantage of separating the truly wise from the terminally stupid, a distinction that is not always apparent among the young.

It is no evolutionary surprise, then, that men retain their reproductive capacity *throughout life*. In the monogamous society, however, the potential for the transmission of accumulated knowledge and proven traits is thwarted, since by the time they come into existence the monogamous same-aged couple is beyond their child-bearing years, and although they may have had some great children, the father's learning has come too late and is wasted; and the opportunity for bearing *more* good children is stymied. And conversely, there are the many women in their forties and fifties who first realize what a loser they had blindly married in their youth; but the damage has already been done with the children they bore with these men still in their callow youth.

In every respect, then, it makes much more sense for young women to mate with *older* men, who will have *proven* their genetic endowment as well as their financial and emotional capacity for raising children. In contrast, the mating of young females with young males is like playing the lottery and hoping for a lucky draw. Few win.

Finally, we must answer this, how can we as a civilization, collectively and as individuals, achieve a much treasured *longevity*—a long, healthy, and rewarding lifespan—if we do not allow for able, productive, and wise men in their seventies, eighties, and nineties to father children with the prime females of the species, passing on their ideal constellation of proven traits for all of posterity. All the surgeons' knives of the world, working in concert for the next 100 years, will not increase the population's projected genetic life expectancy by an hour, in comparison with an enlightened public policy which encourages young females to mate with older men of proven body and mind. To produce and live a good life, we must recognize and mate with a good life. To live to be 100, we must have parents and grandparents who live to be 100.

11. Summary and Conclusions

We began our study of gender differences with the childish question of why girls have long hair and boys have short hair.

After identifying many other gender differences in the context of the reproductive sexual matrix—and synthesizing them into the minimax principle of gender dynamics—we arrived at the important conclusion that polygamy is the natural order among human beings, just as it is in most species of the animal kingdom.

Consistent with this conclusion, we found that institutionalized and ritualized monogamy is responsible for the high incidence of divorce and female grievances in modern society, as well as the genetic de-evolution and behavioral degeneration of civilization as a whole; where the vulgar, banal, and ugly have largely replaced the creative, rewarding and beautiful aspects of human existence. Culture is to blame, and fortunately *culture can be changed*. Mating is the key.

The highlighting of behavioral gender differences has not been done with an aim toward erasing them—for indeed, our thesis is that their underpinnings are genetic in nature and therefore cannot be changed—but rather to unequivocally demonstrate the intrinsic differences between males and females, and hence identify their natural evolutionary roles in a sane society. We found that the differences between males and females are largely qualitative in nature—differing in kind, rather than in any hierarchical sense—and these inborn differences argue for an equal and complementary partnership between males and females in society; where the female's most important lifetime role is to attract a good man and reproduce good children, while the male's main function is to produce for those children, their mothers, and the world community as a whole. These pursuits—along with a recognition of the values of beauty, intelligence, and age—will be inherently and genetically more fulfilling than any of those invented by a superficial and transient society that has lost touch with its origins.

Finally, recognizing that the transition from institutionalized and ritualized monogamy, to a civilization where polygamy can coexist on a parity basis, will be a slow and challenging process—requiring major attitude changes among both males and females, as well as courage to overcome the established regressive forces—let us all, in the meantime, choose our mates as if the future of the world depended upon it.

References

For more information on the basic concepts and analytyical methods referred to in the text, consult the following books:

Darwin, C. (1859). *On the Origin of Species by Means of Natural Selection.* London: John Murray. (Or facsimile editions from Harvard University Press, Cambridge.)

Kachigan, S. K. (1986). *Statistical Analysis: An Interdisciplinary Introduction to Univariate and Multivariate Methods.* New York: Radius Press.

Lüscher, M. (1969). *The Lüscher Color Test* (English translation). New York: Random House.

Wilson, E. O. (1975). *Sociobiology: The New Synthesis.* Cambridge: Belknap Press of Harvard University Press.

Index